TUG OF WAR

A JUDGE'S VERDICT ON SEPARATION,
CUSTODY BATTLES, AND THE
BITTER REALITIES OF FAMILY COURT

BY

THE HONOURABLE MR. JUSTICE
HARVEY BROWNSTONE
ONTARIO COURT OF JUSTICE

Published by ECW Press, 2120 Queen Street East, Suite 200,
Toronto, Ontario, Canada M4E 1E2
416.694.3348 / info@ecwpress.com

LIBRARY AND ARCHIVES CANADA CATALOGUING IN PUBLICATION

Brownstone, Harvey
Tug of war : a judge's verdict on separation, custody battles, and
the bitter realities of family court / Harvey Brownstone.

ISBN 978-1-55022-870-0

1. Domestic relations courts—Canada.
2. Domestic relations—Canada. 3. Custody of children—Canada.
4. Dispute resolution (Law). 5. Divorce mediation—Canada. 1. Title.

KE539.B76 2009   346.7101'50269   C2008-905431-8

Cover and text design: Paul Hodgson
Cover image: Laurent Hamels/PhotoAlto Agency RF Collections/Getty Images
Author photo: Morton Caplan
Typesetting: Mary Bowness
Printing: Webcom

This book is set in Sabon and Avenir.

The publication of *Tug of War* has been generously supported by the Canada Council
for the Arts, which last year invested $20.1 million in writing and publishing through-
out Canada, by the Ontario Arts Council, by the Government of Ontario through
Ontario Book Publishing Tax Credit, by the OMDC Book Fund, an initiative of the
Ontario Media Development Corporation, and by the Government of Canada through
the Book Publishing Industry Development Program (BPIDP).

 Canada Council Conseil des Arts
for the Arts du Canada
 Canadä ONTARIO ARTS COUNCIL
CONSEIL DES ARTS DE L'ONTARIO

PRINTED AND BOUND IN CANADA

ECW PRESS
ecwpress.com

This book is dedicated to my parents,
who raised me in a loving and happy home
and taught me the importance of putting
their child's needs ahead of their own.

And to my extraordinary spouse, Morty,
who has ensured that my only exposure
to marital conflict is professional,
not personal.

TABLE OF CONTENTS

ACKNOWLEDGEMENTS

Everyone knows that behind every curriculum vitae there is another story that paints the true picture of a person. In my case, that story is filled with a great many people who have inspired, nurtured, and encouraged me in all my endeavours and, most recently, in the writing of this book. I extend my deepest love and appreciation to my parents, whose constant love and support has meant the world to me. I also want to thank Morty, my spouse of twenty-four years, who spent many solitary evenings and weekends while I worked on this book. Morty was my muse, collaborator, and trusted adviser. He served as proofreader extraordinaire, tirelessly reading and rereading every word, from the valuable perspective of a non-legally trained person, insisting that the book's content and language be inclusive and accessible by being as easy to understand as possible.

I owe an enormous debt of gratitude to my dear friend and colleague the Honourable Mr. Justice Stanley Sherr, who carefully reviewed the first draft and contributed numerous insights and ideas. Without Stan's input, this book would not be nearly as comprehensive and practical as it is. Moreover, without Stan's unconditional encouragement and support, the process of writing this book would not have been nearly as enjoyable as it was for me.

I also want to express my admiration, respect, and gratitude to my other cherished colleagues at the North Toronto Family Court: the Honourable Justices James Nevins, Marvin Zuker, Geraldine Waldman, Robert Spence, and Carole Curtis. These dedicated family court judges exemplify the highest standards of judicial excellence and have contributed significantly to the themes, case examples, and practical suggestions set out in this book.

I was very fortunate to have had two pivotal experiences as a law student that shaped my legal career. In my first year, I attended a lecture given by Chief Judge Ted Andrews of the Ontario Provincial Court, Family Division (now the Ontario Court of Justice). Chief Judge Andrews displayed an infectious enthusiasm for family law and the work of the family court, and convinced me there and then that I should pursue a career in family law. One of the greatest days of my life occurred eighteen years later when Chief Judge Andrews robed me at my swearing-in ceremony as a judge of the Ontario Court of Justice. Ted very kindly read the manuscript and wrote a wonderful prologue, for which I am extremely grateful. Thank you Ted, for your ongoing inspiration, wisdom, and friendship. You have been an instrumental mentor in my life.

My second pivotal experience as a law student occurred during the summer of 1979, when I was given the unique opportunity to work as a law clerk to the judges at the 311 Jarvis Street family court in Toronto. Judges Rosalie Abella (now a justice of the Supreme Court of Canada), James Karswick, David Main, and Joseph James made a deep and lasting impression on me and shaped my vision of family law justice. They taught me by example that family law is primarily about the best interests of children and that parents must be made aware of the damaging impact on their children of being caught in a toxic tug of war. Justice Abella has inspired me throughout every stage of my career, and she continues to serve as a cherished role model and mentor in more ways than she will ever know. She took the time from her crushing workload and extremely busy schedule to read the manuscript and offer invaluable words of encouragement and support, which means the world to me. And Justice Karswick, who is one of Canada's most respected family court judges and whom I am proud to call a beloved colleague and friend, played an instrumental role in my decision to write this book. I am profoundly grateful for his friendship and guidance, and for the generous foreword he has written.

I have had the extreme good fortune of coming to know and love one of Canada's best-known, admired, and brilliant jurists, Madame Justice Claire L'Heureux-Dubé, who served on the Supreme Court of Canada from 1987 to 2002. Justice L'Heureux-Dubé will forever be known as the "grande dame" of modern Canadian family law because of the many landmark decisions she participated in, which brought numerous progressive reforms to family law jurisprudence. She very graciously agreed to read the manuscript, and provided enthusiastic support not only for the book's message but for the notion that the time has come for family court judges to reach out to the public in the way that I have attempted to do in this book. I thank Claire from the bottom of my heart for her words of wisdom and encouragement, and for the very kind endorsement she has written in support of this book.

I extend my heartfelt thanks to my dear friend and colleague, the Honourable Judge Paula J. Hepner, supervising judge of the family court in Brooklyn, New York. Judge Hepner spent many hours reviewing the manuscript with a view to making the book as applicable as possible to readers in the United States. Her contribution to this book has been invaluable. Her prologue reinforces the fact that regardless of differences between the Canadian and American legal systems, the themes set out in this book apply to all parents and families in conflict.

It touches me deeply that Judith Ryan, one of the world's best known family law lawyers, mediators, and educators, has seen fit to endorse this book as a must-read for family law lawyers and clients. I am honoured and gratified by Judith's words in support of this book's message.

I want to thank Jack David and everyone at ECW Press for their enthusiastic support of this project, as well as my editor, Heather Sangster.

And finally, to all of the lawyers and litigants who have appeared in my court, I want you to know that I have learned something from each and every one of you. I thank you for the honour and privilege of touching your lives, and I hope that at least some of the messages conveyed in this book will ring true for you. My sincere wish is that you will never again have to resort to litigation as a means of resolving family disputes.

Foreword by
CHIEF JUDGE TEDFORD G. ANDREWS (RETIRED), ONTARIO PROVINCIAL COURT, FAMILY DIVISION (NOW THE ONTARIO COURT OF JUSTICE)

I am honoured to have the opportunity to write a foreword to this book. It was written by a judge for whom I have the greatest respect and whom I am truly happy to call my very good friend. Mr. Justice Harvey Brownstone has an uncommon depth of insight into, and a genuine concern for, the adults and children with whom he deals in his daily service in the interests of justice.

The text discloses the inner struggles of parents, lawyers and even judges in the maelstrom of marital conflict. Justice Brownstone's observations are perceptive and comprehensive on the interface between the court and the public who appear before the court. The reader can sense his passion for the subject and his compassion for the parents and children involved in the disputes that come before him.

The writings of this dedicated author are of vital importance to every law student aspiring to be a family law lawyer. Experienced family law lawyers also would benefit from the clarity of defined issues, to update their knowledge and skills. Most urgently this book has messages vitally important for couples and parents who enter the world of new rights and responsibilities following separation.

There are numerous texts written on various aspects of marital conflict by professionals in social work, psychology, psychiatry, and the law, but I know of none written by the key person in the unique and solitary position of observing and analyzing human behaviour and making judgments that will have profound effects on people's lives.

This text is a very valuable contribution. Every lawyer's office should have several copies to offer to clients entering legal spousal conflict.

This book is superbly unique.

It was written by a presiding, experienced, knowledgeable, and caring family court judge who is so touched by the countless families that come into his courtroom that he feels compelled to share his observations, opinions, and recommendations with all who will listen, so that the parental separation and the court experience can be less stressful, less confrontational, and more beneficial, especially for the children. After all, as the Honourable Mr. Justice Brownstone repeatedly points out, it really is, and should be, about the children, our most treasured resource.

Justice Brownstone does not give legal advice — that you should get from a family law lawyer — nor does he give you a detailed, step-by-step methodology for filing court papers and marshalling evidence for the court hearing — that you can get from your lawyer or the many manuals on how to proceed in the family court.

This book prepares you for the emotional impact that separation and court will have on the family and especially upon the children. It points out how, with maturity and a focus on the interests of the children, parents — with the help of professionals and, on occasion, with the help of the family court judge — can negotiate and achieve their own individual and sustainable resolutions.

There are those few cases that simply need to go through the entire family court process. The author discusses those cases and makes many helpful recommendations on how to deal with them in a constructive manner.

Family breakups are increasing, greater numbers of separating parents are reluctant or ashamed to get professional help, and many simply cannot afford to pay a family law lawyer. Consequently the family court judges are having to hear more and more cases where the parents are self-represented.

Obviously, these parents lack the training to present their cases properly, and even if they had that knowledge, the stress and emotion of having to directly confront an ex-partner in a courtroom about the welfare of their children is hardly something any parent is really capable of doing in a rational and focused manner.

Justice Brownstone discusses the fundamental challenges that parents need to address, no matter what the legal rules may be. The challenges facing separating parents and their children transcend geographical, linguistic, and cultural boundaries.

It is the parents, who love their children and know them better than anyone, who are most capable of determining what is best for their children. Remember, it is only the parents caught up in their tug of war who abdicate their responsibility to a stranger — the judge.

As Justice Brownstone reminds us: "Family courts are not in the business of rewarding or punishing anyone, even though there is often a win-lose mentality among litigants — and, unfortunately, even among some misguided lawyers. Everyone should be mindful that there are no winners in family court when the fighting continues — everyone loses, especially the children."

Justice Brownstone's timely work should be read by anyone contemplating separation or going to the family courts.

Indeed, it can be useful to professionals in the field of family law so that they may gain greater insights into the challenges as seen from the perspective of the separating families and as observed by an experienced and talented family court judge.

I have been a family court judge for more than thirty-two years, and still I find this book fascinating, engrossing, and enlightening. I only wish I could have read it twenty years ago because it certainly would have enabled me to be a better, more understanding, and more effective judge.

Foreword by
JUDGE PAULA J. HEPNER, SUPERVISING JUDGE
NEW YORK STATE FAMILY COURT
BROOKLYN, NEW YORK

Justice Harvey Brownstone's book is a powerfully accurate description of the drama that unfolds daily in the courtrooms of judges presiding over child custody and visitation (access) disputes between parents. From his thirteen years of experience hearing and deciding these cases he offers the reader invaluable lessons about what these cases are and are not about and why they become tugs of war and what prevents them from being resolved expeditiously for the sake of the children whose emotional well-being is at stake.

While the book outlines the various stages of a custody or visitation case, Justice Brownstone's purpose is not to write a do-it-yourself manual so parents may feel comfortable representing themselves. On the contrary, Justice Brownstone explains that when parents resort to the courts to decide which parent should have custody of their children, or whether the parent who does not have custody should be able to spend time with the children, they will find themselves in the middle of complex proceedings where unfamiliar legal principles and procedures are applied. These principles and procedures prescribe what information must be presented to the judge, govern the conduct of the case, and determine its outcome.

Justice Brownstone makes it absolutely clear to parents who bring their own custody and visitation battles to the family court that the process is not like going on television to tell their story to the judge, answer some questions, and have it over in fifteen minutes, minus the commercials. With real-life examples carefully selected from cases he has heard, Justice Brownstone illustrates the pitfalls of self-representation by demonstrating where critical mistakes were made or crucial opportunities were missed. In so doing, Justice Brownstone convincingly makes the case that to the maximum extent possible parents should obtain legal counsel or, if hiring an attorney is not feasible, parents should at least obtain legal advice and assistance to help in the preparation and presentation of the case.

This book is also about why these cases take so long to complete, which Justice Brownstone concludes is attributable to immature behaviour. While the laws and legal procedures applicable to custody and visitation cases differ from country to country and jurisdictions within countries, the information contained in this book has universal application for all parents regardless of where they live or where they litigate because parents are human and their behaviour does not vary much from place to place. I am a family court judge sitting in Brooklyn, New York, the busiest family court in the United States. Every single anecdote described in this book is familiar to me. In the past eighteen years, I have encountered each and every one of the parents portrayed in the pages of this book behaving in exactly the same way in my courtroom. For this reason, parents everywhere can learn something extremely important by reading Justice Brownstone's book and taking his message seriously.

It does not matter what child psychologist or psychiatrist one consults or what parenting books or magazines one reads. None will suggest that resorting to the courts to settle issues of custody and visitation is good for the children involved. On the contrary, there is uniformity of opinion that for children, the process of litigation can be extremely damaging. The reason for this is primarily due to the unbelievable stress children experience from being at the centre of their parents' tug of war. Children wait for months, and sometimes years, to learn which parent they are going to live with, while their parents prolong this uncertainty through relentless contretemps of bickering, personal attacks, and obstructionist tactics. To minimize the harm to children, Justice Brownstone describes some alternatives to litigation and explains the benefits of each.

What little civility is left between two parents before walking into court is almost always destroyed by their posturing in the litigation. To reach a decision, judges who preside over these cases need to learn an enormous amount about the parents' lives and their personalities, their stability and judgment, their occupations and work schedules, the roles they have played in their children's lives, and the bonding that exists between parent and child. Almost always, however, the only information parents will present is their list of injustices, portraying each other in the worst possible light: the most abusive, the most irresponsible, the most uninvolved, the most inconsiderate, the most immoral, the most inadequate, the most controlling, the most . . . the most . . . the most. Indeed the majority of parents view the case as *their* chance to get *their* day in court when, in actuality, it is their *children's* day in court. Most parents come to court believing that they are the only two people in the case and that it's all about them when, in fact, it's about those who are not in the room — the children they seem to have forgotten. For parents who did not realize this before, it will become evident very shortly from reading Justice Brownstone's book. Told in the first person and in the form of a personal one-on-one dialogue, this book presents the reader with a chance to hear first-hand from an experienced jurist devoted to the welfare of children how important it is to approach these cases with a mature perspective and a realistic assessment of which parent can meet the children's needs, instead of focusing on how each parent failed to meet the other's needs.

Justice Brownstone speaks for family court judges everywhere in trying to educate parents to focus on what is best for their children. This book will have achieved its purpose if parents can recognize themselves in the pages ahead and can alter their outlook and behaviour so that their children spend much less of their lives being interviewed by social workers, attending psychological evaluations and discussing the case with their lawyers and more time on sports, playing an instrument, or learning computer graphics.

CHAPTER ONE

DO YOU KNOW WHAT YOU'RE GETTING INTO?

AFTER MORE THAN FOURTEEN YEARS OF PRESIDING IN FAMILY COURT, ONE QUESTION HAS NEVER CEASED TO AMAZE ME: how can two parents who love their child allow a total stranger to make crucial decisions about their child's living arrangements, health, education, extracurricular activities, vacation time, and degree of contact with each parent? This question becomes even more mind-boggling when one considers that the stranger making the decisions is a judge, whose formal training is in the law, not in family relations, child development, social work, or psychology. Now add the fact that, because of heavy caseloads and crowded dockets, most judges have to make numerous child custody, access, matrimonial property, and support decisions every day on the basis of incomplete, subjective, and highly emotional written evidence (called *affidavits*), with virtually no time to get to know the parents and no opportunity to meet the child whose life is being so profoundly affected. What person in their right mind would advocate for this method of resolving parental conflicts flowing from family breakdown? These are some of the questions that family court judges agonize over. Some say the answers are complicated and have much to do with social conditioning, economic class, levels of education, sophistication, familiarity with community resources, and even culture. I say the answers are simple.

The institution of marriage has not been a great success in North America. The United States has the highest divorce rate in the western world, followed by the United Kingdom and Canada.[1] Moreover, divorce statistics do not take into account couples who lived in common-law (unmarried) relationships and broke up. There is no reliable way to track the breakup rate for those couples, but you can be sure that it is at least as high as the divorce rate. There are also many thousands of couples who never lived together, but had a casual relationship resulting in the birth of a child. Family courts are heavily populated with such couples, but we have no way of knowing their numbers in society at large.

We do know that the vast majority of couples who break up manage to settle their affairs, including the custody and access arrangements for their children, without ever setting foot in a courtroom. The most common way to achieve this is by separation agreement or some other form of domestic contract (see Chapter 12). However, for the many couples unable to reach agreements, the family court becomes the place of first and last resort.

What we judges see in family court is beyond belief and certainly more dramatic and gut-wrenching than any television show or movie. If you don't believe me, visit any family courtroom in any town and chances are you'll see real-life examples of what I will describe in this book. As any family law lawyer, judge, or litigant will tell you, family court litigation is expensive, time-consuming, unpredictable, and highly stressful. The level of hostility and anger between parents involved in high-conflict custody disputes is often so toxic that it is almost palpable. I have dealt with thousands of couples whose bitterness toward each other coloured every aspect of the proceedings and completely diverted the focus away from the children and their needs. Frequently, I get the impression that such parents are in a struggle over power and control or are on a quest for vengeance and self-validation that has nothing to do with their children. Imagine how difficult it is for a judge to make the best possible decision regarding a child's living arrangements when faced with parents who seem unable or unwilling to focus on their children. Sometimes I have had to involve a child protection agency and place the children in foster care to insulate them from the parental conflict (see Chapter 11). On more than one occasion I have been told by a parent that he/she would rather have his/her children living in foster care than with the other parent. On one even more appalling occasion, I was told by a parent that it would be better for the children to be dead than to live with the other parent! This is the tragic reality of family court.

Everyone who works in family law, including judges, agrees on two things: family court is not good for families, and litigation is not good for children. The emotional carnage resulting from family litigation, and its impact on the unfortunate children of warring parents, cannot be overstated. And yet, family courts everywhere are jammed with couples asking judges to decide who gets custody of their children, how often the children will see the noncustodial parent, how the matrimonial property is to be divided, and how much spousal and/or child support must be paid. More surprisingly, an alarmingly high number of people appear in court without a lawyer and try to navigate the court process on their own, without any idea of their rights and obligations, the procedural requirements, the rules of evidence, or the types of orders a court can and cannot make. As you might expect, the results for these people are often extremely frustrating at best and disastrous at worst.

Ask anyone who has ever appeared in family court as a litigant — even if they had a lawyer — and they are almost certain to describe their experience as unsatisfactory. Why? What can be done to help people so that their family court experience is more predictable, more positive and constructive, less time-consuming, and consequently more beneficial to themselves and their children? An even more important question is, What can be done to help people avoid going to court in the first place? That is what I am going to explain in this book.

What is the difference between the couples who settle their disputes privately and those couples who require a judge to make the decisions? Do the parents in the first group dislike each other any less than those in the second group? Does the first group have access to resources unavailable to the second group? Do the two groups come from separate and distinct socio-economic or cultural groups? Not in my experience. In my opinion, the major difference between couples who resolve their disputes privately and those who turn to a judge has to do with one overriding characteristic: *maturity*. We who work in family court know that a person's maturity level has nothing to do with economic circumstances, education, culture, race, religion, or sexual orientation. We see rich people and poor people in our courtrooms, and we see people from all walks of life and from every racial, cultural, ethnic, and religious background, and from every lifestyle and orientation imaginable. Trust me: judges see it all. What we *don't* see very often in our clientele is maturity.

In the context of a relationship breakdown, being mature means loving your children more than you dislike your ex-partner. Being mature means caring enough about your children that you will force yourself to deal in a civilized way with someone you may hate. Being mature means thinking twice and measuring your words carefully before you shoot your mouth off when you're upset with your ex-partner, especially in front of the children. It means always insulating your children from parental conflict so they know your breakup has nothing to do with them. It means doing what is necessary to make the transition in your children's lives as easy for them as possible. Being mature means putting your children's needs ahead of your own. It means truly understanding and accepting that your children are entitled to love and be loved by *both* of their parents. It means giving your children emotional permission to express and receive that love, even though you and the other parent dislike each other. Being mature means being willing and able to reach compromises so that your children can have peace rather than be caught in a tug of war and conflict of loyalties. Being mature means recognizing that you can be an ex-partner but you are never going to be an ex-parent. True maturity requires parents to appreciate that children need both parents in their lives, working co-operatively to make the best possible decisions for their upbringing.

In my experience, mature people fully understand that even though they no longer love each other, they are the most qualified people to make important decisions for their children. After all, parents know their children best. Children deserve to have parents working together as a team in all matters affecting their welfare. Mature people do not give up their parental decision-making responsibilities to a total stranger, even if that stranger wears a robe and is called "Your Honour."

The purpose of this book is to help separated and divorced parents, as well as parents who never lived together, conduct themselves with the maturity their children need and deserve, so they can resolve parenting conflicts in a civilized and proactive way, hopefully without court involvement. I believe that maturity of perspective and behaviour can be taught and that sufficiently motivated people can learn to adapt to their circumstances and alter their way of approaching difficult situations. I have found that most parents love their children enough to become motivated to adopt a mature course of conduct in dealing with ex-partners. The motivation comes once they understand the impact of their immature behaviour on their children's well-being. I know this is true because every day my colleagues and I help couples to shift their perspectives and take a child-focused approach to the resolution of family disputes. In the vast majority of cases, we see positive results, and parents emerge from the process with a mutually agreeable parenting plan, although it is fair to say that most ex-partners emerge from the court process emotionally bruised and not very happy with each other, and often not very happy with the judge!

It has always bothered me that family court judges don't get the opportunity to offer this help until far too much damage has already been done. We don't see parents until they and their lawyers are seated in our courtrooms geared up for the battle of their lives. The task of the family court judge is difficult at that stage, because instead of looking forward, parents mostly want to look back. We should be trying to construct a co-operative, co-parenting regime that is in the children's best interests. Instead, we spend a great deal of time trying to de-escalate the hostilities and refocus the parties away from their litany of complaints against each other. Separated couples seem to relish the prospect of rehashing every bad thing that each party did to the other throughout the entire course of the relationship. Many people apparently need to hear the judge validate their perceived victimization. While this may have a therapeutic effect for the parents (and that is questionable, as judges are not trained therapists), it mostly serves to reopen old wounds and create new ones. Most importantly, it does not help the judge decide what is best for the children.

What if parents headed for family court could hear from the judge before they got there? What if they knew what to expect (and equally importantly, what *not* to expect) from the court process, and also what the court expects from them? What if they knew the alternatives to court litigation so they could choose the dispute resolution process that best suits their needs and circumstances? I believe that informed parents make better decisions than uninformed parents. This book is intended to provide separated parents with much-needed information and insights, so they can make the most informed and best decisions *before* they decide to "tell it to the judge" — or better yet, so they won't ever have to surrender their joint decision-making powers to a judge. If you apply the principles set out in this book, it is my hope you will never need to go to family court. Even if you do find yourself facing the prospect of a family court case, the suggestions in this book will help you, your ex-partner, and your respective lawyers to maximize your chances for a child-focused and mutually beneficial resolution to your parental dispute.

I am often asked how the maturity rule would apply in extremely difficult situations. How would it work for couples who have experienced domestic violence or when a parent has a mental health problem or a substance abuse problem? What if a parent's conduct has exposed a child to a risk of harm, neglect, or abuse? What if one parent is refusing to provide the other with full details of his/her finances so that property and support issues can't be settled? The answer, quite simply, is that conducting yourself in a mature fashion when dealing with the other parent does *not* necessarily mean that the other parent gets everything he/she wants. Where you can prove with credible evidence that one of the above circumstances exists, you may need to go to court. The court can make a *restraining order* (sometimes called a *protection order*), or an order for a psychiatric assessment, drug testing, or to obtain financial disclosure, or to have certain restrictions and limitations imposed on a parent's contact with a child. The court can certainly be a necessary and useful resource in difficult cases, but going to court does not relieve a parent of the obligation to act maturely.

You must keep in mind that all court cases — even the extremely difficult ones — eventually come to an end. It is important to understand and accept that in all but the most severe cases of abuse, most parents will still have to deal with each other regarding custody and access of their children. The parent-child relationship will continue, even if in a limited way. Even if your ex-partner is hospitalized, in a drug rehabilitation facility, in jail, or on probation with a no-contact condition (see Chapter 10), he/she will almost certainly be looking to re-establish contact with the child when these circumstances change. Whether you like it or not, this will necessitate at least some form of contact with you. So I believe that the maturity rule still applies in these cases — perhaps even more so, given the special challenges that come with having an ex-partner with special needs.

You and your ex-partner are the only biological or adoptive parents your children will ever have, and you are their role models. It is important to their well-being that you develop and maintain the best possible relationship with your ex-partner. You must do all you can to bring out the best you and your ex-partner have to offer your children, not the worst. You, your ex-partner, and your children can only benefit from your taking a calm, reasonable, and child-focused approach to your parenting issues, even if the other parent is not behaving that way. The court will always be more favourably impressed with maturity than with immaturity, regardless of how the other parent is conducting himself or herself.

Judges have traditionally refrained from making themselves available to the public other than in the courtroom. It is generally felt that judges should remain outside the fray of public debate on social and political issues, so as to maintain their impartiality. Many judges believe they should express themselves only through their court decisions and written judgments and not by way of letters to the editor, media interviews, public-speaking engagements, and books, at least not until they have retired from the judiciary. I definitely agree that judges must be cautious to avoid controversial or political issues and should never comment on specific ongoing cases or offer legal advice.

With those parameters in mind, however, I strongly believe that judges have a public role to play outside the courtroom. I believe we have a social obligation to be educators as well as adjudicators. We have a unique role in society that offers us a golden opportunity to enlighten the public on many aspects of the justice system and, where appropriate, to advocate for improvements to the accessibility of justice for all. I believe that this social obligation is particularly applicable to family court judges, given the widespread family breakdown in society and its devastating impact on parents and children, and given the equally widespread dissatisfaction experienced by family court litigants. Family court work is the most important work that judges do, because it deals with the best interests of children, who are society's most precious resource. And so, after more than fourteen years of presiding in family court and thinking about how best to help separated parents and their children *before* they embark on a potentially destructive "voyage of no return" through the court system, I decided to write this book. If you and your children benefit, even in a small way, from the heartfelt suggestions I have made, I will have accomplished something worthwhile.

A note of caution: this book is not intended to provide legal advice, nor is it a substitute for having your own lawyer. No book can replace the individualized, case-specific, strategic advice and representation that your own lawyer can give you, because every family's circumstances require a unique approach tailored to their specific issues and needs. Nor is this a legal textbook or self-help manual to guide you through every step of the family justice system. In fact, this book does not cover every legal issue that can arise after a separation. Family law varies greatly from one jurisdiction to the next, making it impossible to generalize. For example, in some jurisdictions, married couples are treated differently than unmarried couples, and same-sex couples are treated differently than opposite-sex couples.

Throughout this book, I have provided many hypothetical situations and real case histories from Canadian courts to illustrate legal principles. These examples are not intended to provide legal advice. Please be aware that each case is unique and must be decided on its own facts and according to the applicable law of the jurisdiction in question. Even though you may think that your situation is similar to a case example in this book, it may not be. Moreover, the law where you live may not be the same as the law that was applied in the case examples. Therefore, do not assume that the results in any given situation will be the same as those in the book's case examples. Only a family law lawyer can tell you how the law in your area applies to your specific circumstances.

Although some reference is made to financial issues such as child support, the primary focus of this book is *custody* and *access* (sometimes called *visitation*) of children. This is because the law dealing with matrimonial property and financial matters arising from family breakdown is different in each jurisdiction. More importantly, I believe that the resolution of parenting issues is far more crucial to the overall welfare of children than the settling of financial and property issues.

In this book I have endeavoured to lay the foundation for an emotional blueprint to help you establish and sustain a positive and constructive mindset to approach the resolution of parenting conflicts, particularly if you plan to access the court system. The book explains the roles that lawyers and courts play in helping parents resolve their post-separation conflicts, and offers alternative methods of dispute resolution. It explains what you can expect from the family justice system and, equally importantly, what the system expects from you. It dispels many commonly held myths and misconceptions that so frequently stand in the way of peace and co-operation between separated parents. The book also sounds warning signals to help you identify and avoid the pitfalls many parents encounter in family litigation.

If you take to heart the information and insights I have tried to impart in the following chapters, you will have realistic and practical expectations of what your lawyer and the family justice system can and cannot do for you. You may even be able to negotiate a parenting plan that will eliminate the need to go to court. And even if you do end up in court, you will at the very least minimize the potential emotional damage to yourself and your children. I believe this is true even if your ex-partner does not behave in a reasonable or child-focused way. It takes two to keep a dispute alive, and especially to keep a court action going.[2] It is my sincere hope that by adopting the approach I advocate in this book, you will be doing all you can to reduce and resolve parental conflicts in a way that positions you and your ex-partner to be child-focused co-parents for the duration of your children's childhoods.

---

1   Anne-Marie Ambert, "Divorce: Facts, Figures and Consequences," Vanier Institute of the Family Web site at **www.vifamily.ca/library/cft/divorce_05.html#Children**. For more information about divorce rates in Canada, go to the Statistics Canada Web site at **www.statcan.ca/Daily/English/040504/d040504a.htm**. For information about divorce rates in the United States, go to the National Center for Health Statistics Web site at **www.cdc.gov/nchs/fastats/divorce.htm**. For information about divorce rates in other countries, see the Divorce Magazine Web site at **www.divorcemag.com/statistics/statsWorld.shtml**.

2   This is not always true. In a small but very problematic category of cases, it can take just one obsessively relentless party to keep a dispute and court action going indefinitely. In most jurisdictions, the law provides ways to stop a person from continually bringing frivolous and vexatious court actions. If you feel you are being victimized by a persistent litigant, consult a lawyer.

CHAPTER TWO

WHY FAMILY COURT SHOULD BE THE LAST RESORT

MOST SEPARATED COUPLES NEVER SET FOOT INSIDE A COURT-ROOM.[1] Sometimes they have agreed on their financial and property issues and their parenting plan and don't need anyone's help. In my experience, very few couples fall into this category. Ask yourself how many separated couples you know who were able to agree on every issue from the outset on their own without professional assistance. I doubt you would know very many. If you did, there wouldn't be so many family law lawyers!

Most separated couples have major disagreements about financial matters or the custody of their children, and still the great majority do not go to court. I believe this is because they understand that family court should be the option of last resort rather than the first place to run to, which is the approach too many people take. It may seem inconsistent that, on the one hand, I have said that most separated couples do not go to court, while on the other hand I am saying that too many people go to court. The fact is that both statements are true. That is, while less than 10 per cent of separated couples go to family court to resolve their problems,[2] this figure represents a very large number of people. That is why family courts everywhere are so busy and some are experiencing unprecedented and ever-increasing backlogs.

You may also find it odd that a judge, whose very livelihood depends on people bringing their disputes to court, would be trying to dissuade you from going to court. The truth is that family court judges have more than enough work just dealing with child protection cases (where a child protection agency has removed neglected or abused children from their parents) and youth criminal justice (in some jurisdictions called *juvenile delinquency*) matters (in which a child has been charged with committing a criminal offence). Plus, as explained in Chapter 3, there will always be some couples whose circumstances necessitate court action. So I have no fear of losing my job for lack of work. My point is that *most* couples who bring their disputes to family court do not need to and do not enjoy, or ultimately benefit from, the experience. I would go further and suggest that in many cases, the parties' ability to communicate and co-operate with each other as co-parents became worse, not better, as a result of family court litigation.

What's wrong with going to court?

Why is litigation such a damaging and destructive way to resolve parental disputes? The answer is simple: the court system is based on an adversarial process in which "winning" is the object of the exercise. Parents who should be on the same team for their children's sake become hostile adversaries in a courtroom. They focus all of their attention and efforts on emphasizing each other's shortcomings and failings over the life of the relationship. Some people point out that in recent years, efforts have been made by lawmakers and courts to soften the rules and treat family law cases with more humanity and sensitivity than other lawsuits. However, the fact remains that family litigation is still litigation, and any lawyer or judge will tell you that a lawsuit is a most unpleasant and highly competitive way to resolve a dispute. If the parties to a lawsuit have to keep dealing with each other for many more years, as is the case with parents, the effects of litigation on their ability to do so amicably can be tragic and long-lasting. Believe me when I tell you that litigation is not a friendly exercise. But that is not the only reason why it should be avoided whenever possible.

How family court works: the importance of motions and temporary orders

In order to understand why litigation is undesirable, it is necessary to know how family court works. In a court case, each party presents the evidence he/she has to support the conclusion he/she wants the judge to reach. This evidence usually takes the form of sworn affidavits, business records, and expert reports (such as medical reports or property valuations). If a trial is being held, the judge would also hear the testimony of the parties and their witnesses. Trials rarely occur because they are expensive (imagine paying a lawyer $500 per hour for a five-day trial in addition to paying for the lawyer's many hours of preparation time), and caseload backlogs cause long delays in booking trial time in most courts.

Most family law cases are decided by way of motions, which are hearings for temporary orders, conducted solely on the basis of the written evidence mentioned above, not oral testimony from witnesses. In a motion, the judge makes a decision after reading the written evidence and listening to the parties' (hopefully their lawyers') oral arguments. The judge's decision becomes a temporary court order, which will determine the custodial and financial arrangements that will exist until the case ends. Although orders made at motions are supposed to be temporary, they usually last a long time because family court litigation moves slowly due to the time needed to negotiate settlements — and of course, those court backlogs mentioned above. Consequently in most cases, temporary orders establish a settled state of affairs (referred to as a *status quo*) that can be hard to disrupt by the time the parties are ready to have a trial. For this reason, orders obtained on motions can have a huge and often determinative impact on the final result in the case.

For example, assume that soon after a separation, Parent A and Parent B go to family court to litigate the issues of custody, access, and child support. After conducting a motion, the judge makes a temporary order granting custody to Parent A, with access to Parent B on alternate weekends and one evening during the week. Parent B is also ordered to pay monthly child support. Over the next six months, the parties' lawyers attempt to negotiate a final settlement, but the parents fail to reach agreement on the key issue of custody because each parent wants the child to live with him/her. A trial is scheduled to occur one year after the temporary order was made. The fact that the child will have been in Parent A's sole custody for an entire year by the time the trial occurs will be a very important factor for the court to consider in deciding custody, especially if the child has been doing well in Parent A's care. This is because courts try hard not to disrupt children's living arrangements and to maintain as much stability and consistency in their lives as possible (see Chapter 6).

How cases end

Cases usually end in one of three ways: (1) a trial is held (which is very rare), (2) one or both parties withdraws from the case or simply stops participating in it and is deemed to have abandoned it (usually because he/she is financially and/or emotionally drained and has decided to "give up"), (3) the parties have negotiated a resolution to the dispute, in which case the court will usually make a final order in the terms of their agreement.

Sadly, there is a fourth way a case can end, and I have seen it far too many times: the parents keep litigating for so long that the child in question grows up and becomes an adult. Imagine two parents spending the entire duration of their child's childhood in litigation, bringing motion after motion against each other — usually to change or enforce terms of custody and access orders. I regularly see parents starting court motions at the slightest infraction or provocation by the other parent. Examples abound: a child was not delivered for an access visit with enough clothing; an item of clothing was not returned after an access visit (or was returned unwashed); a child's toy has gone missing; a parent was a few minutes late for an access exchange; a child missed a nap during an access visit; and the list goes on. I have even seen parents litigate over the length and style of their child's hair, or the brand of toothpaste the child should use. What a way to raise a child! Think of the time, energy, and money wasted by these parents on their never-ending tit-for-tat battles. More importantly, think of what children caught in the middle of these battles must go through. Someday I am sure that one of the unfortunate children who has lived through such a nightmare will write a book about it, and it will be a far more potent and chilling horror story than anything dreamed up by a fiction writer.

Evidence and the judge

By now it should be clear that motions are the most important hearings in family court. Remember that these decisions are made on the basis of *written* evidence, not oral testimony from the parents and their witnesses. The judge's role is to determine the legal admissibility of the evidence, and then decide the issue in question. The rules of evidence are complex, and litigants are often astounded to find that the court will not accept certain items of evidence (such as letters, voice recordings, videos, and photographs) because the technical requirements for admissibility have not been met.

Moreover, many people are shocked to learn that certain incidents they consider to be crucial are completely ignored by the judge because in law they are irrelevant. For example, in custody cases many parents want the judge to deny the other parent contact with the child because of conduct that has nothing to do with the parent-child relationship, such as marital infidelity or financial circumstances. A ruling of inadmissibility can be enormously frustrating and confusing for parents desperate to present their case to the judge. This is one of the most important reasons why people need the help of a lawyer (see Chapter 5).

How judges make decisions

Family court judges make decisions by examining the *admissible* evidence that has been presented and applying the balance of probabilities test (in some jurisdictions, this is called the *preponderance of the evidence*). This test requires the judge to decide how much importance to attach to each item of evidence and then make findings of fact on the basis of what is *most likely to be true*. If some allegation is considered more likely than not to be true, then on a balance of probabilities, that fact will be accepted as true. In other words, if an allegation is *probably* true, then on a balance of probabilities, it will be found to be true for the purposes of judicial fact-finding. For example, if one parent accuses the other parent of hitting the child, the judge will review all of the evidence and decide whether it is more likely than not that (1) the child was hit and (2) that the perpetrator was the parent in question. *Proof on a balance of probabilities is not the same standard of proof as that applied in criminal court.* The standard of proof in criminal court is "proof beyond a reasonable doubt," which requires a much higher degree of certainty than proof on a balance of probabilities. Sometimes the criminal court and the family court can reach opposite conclusions about the same incident, as happened in the O.J. Simpson murder case. In criminal court, Simpson was acquitted of murder because the jury was not satisfied beyond a reasonable doubt that he killed the victims. But in the civil lawsuit filed by the victims' families, Simpson was found liable to pay damages for killing the victims because the jury was convinced on a balance of probabilities that he killed the victims.

The same thing often happens with recently separated couples, especially in cases where domestic violence is alleged. For example, a parent can be facing a criminal charge for assaulting the other parent, while at the same time the parents can be litigating in family court. Amazingly, the two courts can (and sometimes do) make contradictory findings regarding the same incident. (See Chapter 11 for a complete discussion of what happens when parents are involved in both criminal and family court.)

It can be challenging for family court judges to make factual findings, because most parents we see have totally opposite versions of every incident they ever lived through! We spend our days listening to "he said, she said" and sometimes end up believing neither party. Who knows what really happened? Maybe the truth lies somewhere in between both parties' versions. Each case must be looked at on its own merits, but obviously the task of credibility assessment and fact-finding is not an exact science, and judges are only human. We do our best with the evidence we're given, but we have no illusions about the frailties of the court process when it comes to determining the facts, assessing parenting skills, and making the best possible decisions for children.

Court cases are supposed to be truth-finding exercises, but litigants quickly learn that cases are not decided on the basis of what actually happened — a judge cannot know for certain what actually happened because he/she was not there to see it. The best we can do is to make decisions on the basis of what can be *proved*. For example, if you want the judge to find as a fact that your ex-partner is a drug addict, it will probably not be good enough to simply write an affidavit to this effect. If your ex-partner denies the allegation, the judge is left with your word against your ex-partner's. The judge will be looking for the best, most reliable *proof* of your ex-partner's substance abuse problem (for example, police reports, hair or urine drug screen results, reports from doctors or drug counsellors — all of which may be available by court order — and possibly affidavits from others who have witnessed the drug use). Without objective and impartial evidence from reliable sources, the judge may not be satisfied on a balance of probabilities that the fact you are alleging is true — or, to be more accurate, probably true — even if you know it is true.

Just in case you were wondering, neither you nor your ex-partner, nor any relatives or friends, can truly be considered objective and impartial. The parties to a lawsuit and all persons who are in non-arm's length relationships with them can hardly be considered unbiased or objective. And while I'm at it, you should know that in many jurisdictions, family court judges almost never meet the children in a custody case. It is generally believed that children can be put at risk of emotional harm by being pressured into choosing between their parents. In some jurisdictions the court may appoint a lawyer (sometimes called a *law guardian* or *guardian ad litem*) for a child who is old enough to express his/her wishes. There is also the possibility of ordering a best interests assessment to be conducted by a qualified psychologist or social worker. However, even if the judge agrees to meet privately with the child (a common practice in some places), it is almost unheard of for the child to testify in a custody or access case, and that is how it should be. Imagine how horrible it would be for your child to be cross-examined in front of a judge by your lawyer or your ex-partner's lawyer. What loving parent would put their child through such an ordeal? (For more about obtaining and assessing children's wishes in custody and access disputes, see Chapter 6.)

The court is not bound by the parents' options

If your head isn't already spinning, there's more. One factor that parents rarely consider in custody and access cases is that the judge is not restricted to accepting either parent's plan. Frequently, the judge disagrees with *both* parents and constructs a parenting arrangement that is a compromise between both plans, or something completely original. For example, Parent A may want the children to live with him/her and spend alternate weekends and every Wednesday evening with

Parent B. Parent B may want the children to live with him/her and spend alternate weekends and every Wednesday evening with Parent A. It is possible that after carefully considering all of the circumstances, the court may decide that the children should live with Parent A from Sunday evening to Wednesday evening and with Parent B for the rest of the week. Are you prepared to take the risk of something like this happening? Is the dispute between you and your ex-partner so bitter and out of control that you would willingly surrender your joint decision-making authority to a complete stranger who doesn't know you or your children and who will not have to live with the consequences of his/her decision? Of course, my colleagues and I try our best, but you need to know before you embark on a court case that we are not really equipped to know what's best for your family.

In extreme cases, of which I have certainly seen my fair share, the court not only rejects the plan of each parent but decides that *neither* parent is a suitable caregiver, resulting in the child being placed in foster care. Remember, if you and your ex-partner are making serious accusations of parental unfitness against each other, the judge has to decide whom, if anyone, to believe. If the judge should happen to believe you both, and finds that neither parent is fit to have custody, you and your ex-partner will walk out of the courtroom with no children! So many parents treat custody cases as if they were games or contests to see who can trash the other parent the most. Beware, and understand that if you are going to play that game, the stakes are high. Don't accuse the other parent of misconduct or parental unfitness unless it is true *and* you can prove it — and remember that the judge has the power to call in the local child protection authorities, who could remove your child from both of you. (For a complete discussion of the intervention by child protection agencies in custody and access disputes, see Chapter 11.)

After the court case ends

In most custody cases, one parent will obtain a custody order (for a discussion of joint custody, see Chapter 7) and will see him/herself as the "winner." This never ceases to amaze me, because from where I sit, I can assure you that I have never seen a "winner" in family court. Everyone loses, especially the children. And what happens after one parent "wins"? Does the bickering and fighting end after the court has made its decision? Do the parties forgive each other and forget all of the mudslinging that occurred? Not very likely. Even decades after their court cases end, many people find themselves still unable to let go of the hurt they feel because of what their ex-partners said and did during the litigation.

There's even more bad news: court costs. In most jurisdictions, the law requires the unsuccessful party (the parent whose claim was rejected by the court) to pay at least a portion of the legal fees of the successful party (the parent whose claim was granted by the court).[3] That is one of the only ways the law can encourage litigants to be reasonable in their litigation strategy. The portion payable may be as high as 100 per cent of the successful party's costs, depending on the circumstances. You must always remember that judges are in the justice business, not the vengeance business. Ex-spouses who want to litigate "for the principle of the matter" are likely going to pay a very high cost for those principles if they lose, because they will have to pay the other party's legal fees in addition to their own. So, if you want to launch a claim against the other party for custody, access, a restraining order, support, property division, or anything else, you should only do so after being advised by a family law lawyer that your claim has merit. It should also go without saying that your lawyer should conduct the litigation in such a way as to avoid delays or unnecessary expenses for either side.

After the court case is over and the costs have been paid, can you be really sure that it is over? Of course not! There is always the threat of an appeal by the unsuccessful party. Appeals in family law cases are not as common as in other types of cases, but they do occur — and when they do, they compound the parties' hostilities, stress, legal costs, and unhappiness. Most importantly, they prolong children's anxiety and uncertainty about which parent they will live with and when they will see their other parent.

Quite apart from appeals, there is always the prospect of a parent commencing a fresh court action to vary the order if circumstances have changed since it was made. Family court orders involving children are never truly final. Some parents are unwilling or unable to be flexible as the children grow and change their routines. Parents who cannot reach agreements to adjust visitation schedules to accommodate work hours, the children's extracurricular activities, vacation times, and so forth find themselves returning to court many times to seek variations of the custody and access order. I am always bewildered that, despite the widespread dissatisfaction with the court system expressed by family court litigants, many seem to be eager to return to court frequently to start the whole process again! I have some cases in which I know the people so well that I feel like a member of the family! (For more about appeals and requests to change court orders, see Chapter 12.)

Summary

Are you beginning to see why a courtroom is a less-than-ideal place to resolve parental disputes? Let's review all of the reasons to consider an alternative form of dispute resolution:

1) Lawyers' fees are expensive.
2) Courts are often backlogged, and there can be delays in getting your case before a judge.
3) The judge will be making crucial decisions about your children by way of motion, without ever hearing you testify, unless you are one of the very few who litigate all the way to trial.
4) The judge will probably never hear directly from your children.
5) If you are like most litigants I see, it is likely that a lot of the evidence you would want to put before the court will be rejected because it is inadmissible or irrelevant.
6) It is also probable that the evidence offered by your relatives and friends will not be considered impartial or objective and may not be accorded the weight you feel it deserves.
7) Because the judge has the exclusive authority to decide what is in your child's best interests, and because he/she is not bound by the parents' proposals, you run a very real risk that neither parent's plan will be accepted and that the judge will devise his/her own parenting plan, which may appeal to you less than the plan that was proposed by your ex-partner.
8) The unsuccessful party may be required to pay some or all of the successful party's legal fees in addition to his/her own legal fees.

9) There is always the possibility of an appeal, which imposes more delays, costs, and uncertainties.

10) Even after a custody and access order has been made, a fresh court case can be started to change that order if a material change in circumstances has occurred.

For all those reasons, it is imperative that you consider all your options and not simply run to court as a knee-jerk reaction the moment you and your ex-partner have a disagreement.

---

1   It is necessary to file court papers to obtain a divorce. However, because no-fault divorce exists almost everywhere, almost every divorce is granted on a consent or uncontested basis, without the parties ever appearing before a judge. In other words, most divorces are granted without the parties litigating against each other to resolve any disputed issues.

2   There do not appear to be reliable statistics tracking the percentage of separated couples who resort to litigation to resolve their family law issues. This is partly because there is no way to track the number of unmarried couples who break up. The 10 per cent figure referred to is an anecdotal estimate based on my conversations with family law specialist lawyers in Canada and the United States. There appears to be a consensus among these lawyers that only 10 per cent of their caseloads require family court litigation or private arbitration; the rest of their cases are settled by way of separation agreements, using traditional inter-lawyer negotiations, mediation, or the collaborative law process (see Chapter 4).

3   It is recognized that if one or both parties are represented by government-funded legal counsel, there may be no cost consequences for taking an unreasonable position in the litigation. The question of whether and to what extent a party represented by government-funded legal counsel can be ordered to pay the other party's legal costs depends on the applicable legislation in each jurisdiction.

CHAPTER THREE

WHEN GOING TO COURT IS NECESSARY

AS MENTIONED IN CHAPTER 1, THERE ARE SOME CIRCUMSTANCES WHERE IT IS NECESSARY TO START A COURT ACTION, REGARDLESS OF A PARENT'S MATURE ATTITUDE AND BEHAVIOUR, AND NO MATTER HOW MUCH HE/SHE WOULD LIKE TO AVOID LITIGATION. You may have to go to court if your ex-partner is refusing to communicate or is being unreasonable — for example, by evicting you from your home, keeping the children from you, or emptying your bank account. You should always consult a family law lawyer before deciding how to resolve a dispute with your ex-partner, as a lawyer is the most qualified person to advise you. If your lawyer advises that a court action is necessary, you should follow that advice.

In addition to the above scenarios, the following are the most common situations in which court action will always be appropriate.

Refusal to provide financial disclosure

In cases involving the division of matrimonial property or financial matters such as spousal and child support, the law requires the parties to provide each other with complete details of their finances. This is called *providing financial disclosure*. At the very least, thorough financial statements supported by income tax documents are almost always required. Depending on the circumstances, one or both parties may have to provide documents relating to income (salary, self-employed earnings, rental income, insurance proceeds, investment income, and so on), property (land, vehicles, personal property, bank accounts, investments, pensions, and so on), expenses and debts (mortgage and loan applications and statements, credit card statements, and so on). If a party has an interest in a corporation, he/she may be required to produce financial statements and other records of the corporation. Where child support is being paid, the obligation to disclose annual income generally lasts for the duration of the support obligation (see Chapter 12).

Obviously, a fair settlement cannot be reached on any property or financial issue unless full and frank financial disclosure has been provided. If a party is refusing to provide complete financial disclosure, the other party will have to start a court case to obtain it. The court can specify the documents that must be disclosed and set timelines for this to be done. If the order is not obeyed, the law in each jurisdiction permits the court to make a variety of enforcement orders, such as costs awards or findings of contempt of court. If you are involved in a case involving property or financial matters, consult a family law lawyer to advise you on what financial disclosure you will need to give and receive. Your lawyer will also know whether it will be necessary to go to court to obtain full disclosure from your ex-partner.

Domestic violence
Emergency temporary restraining orders

Where a person has been assaulted or threatened by his/her partner,[1] it is important to consider seeking a restraining order (sometimes called a *protection order*) from the family court. Whether or not the police have been called, and regardless of whether criminal charges have been laid, a person who has good reason to fear his/her partner or ex-partner should consult a lawyer about the possibility of bringing an emergency court motion. If the applicant can show that the other party's conduct also poses a threat to the children, the restraining order can include them as well. The family court can also make an emergency temporary custody order if it is in the best interests of the children.

A restraining order is a court order either prohibiting or severely limiting a person's right to have contact or communication with one or more persons. The order may also set out a number of locations where the person is not to go. For example, Parent A may be restrained from going within 500 metres of Parent B's home or place of employment. If the court finds that Parent A constitutes a threat to the safety of the children, the order may restrain him/her from being in the vicinity of the children's school, daycare centre, or any other place where the children regularly go.

As you might expect, restraining orders can be problematic because they are almost always brought on an urgent basis without notice to the other party. This is called bringing an *ex parte* motion. In such motions, the court has to decide whether to make the order solely by reading the applicant's evidence without the benefit of getting the other party's side of the story. There is an obvious risk of injustice whenever a court is making a decision with only one side of the story, because everyone knows that there are always at least two sides to every story. Nevertheless, the justice system must provide a way to protect people whose safety is at risk in an emergency. Because the order is made without notice to the other party, it will be a temporary order and will last only until the next court date, which in most cases will be a few weeks after the order is made.

Prior to the next court date, the applicant will be required to have the order, together with all of the court documents, given to the other party. This is called *serving* the other party. Most jurisdictions require that the papers be physically handed to the person (this is called *personal service*), unless the court permits service to be done by mail, courier, or some other way. The applicant should not be the one to serve the other party personally because there may be too great a risk to the applicant's safety, depending on the other party's likely reaction to the order. Besides, if the court has just made an order prohibiting someone from coming near you, you should not be putting that person in a position to violate the order. Depending on the law where you live, it may be possible to have a relative or friend serve the documents. The best and most reliable way to serve the other party is to hire a process server or bailiff because these professionals know how to get the job done. Sometimes it is necessary to hire a private investigator to locate the person. In some jurisdictions, the family court can arrange for a court officer or sheriff to serve the court documents. The best person to ask about how to serve the documents is a lawyer.

Once the other party has been served with the court papers, he/she will have an opportunity to prepare a response that will be served on you and filed with the court. On the next court date, the judge will review both parties' evidence and decide whether the restraining order should continue in effect, be modified, or terminated.

Although most restraining orders are made on an emergency basis without notice to the other party, it is not always necessary to do it that way. In some circumstances, it is appropriate to serve the other party with the motion in advance of the court date. For example, if the other party is in jail and not likely to be released in the next few days, there is no emergency to justify proceeding to court behind his/her back. It is only fair that he/she be given notice of the motion, so that he/she may arrange for a lawyer to prepare a written response and appear in court on his/her behalf at the motion. The best and only way to know whether an emergency motion should be brought is to get legal advice from a family law lawyer.

If you are going to bring an emergency motion without notice to the other party, the law in most jurisdictions requires you to meet two requirements:

1) You must give the court compelling evidence of misconduct by the other party (such as an assault or threat to cause harm) that would give you good reason to be fearful for your safety and/or the safety of your children. For example, the evidence might include police reports showing domestic violence, medical records describing injuries, affidavits from witnesses who have seen the misconduct, and photographs of property damage; *and*

2) You must also satisfy the court that there is such an emergency that it would not be reasonable or practical to give the other party advance notice of the motion.

A motion for a restraining order brought behind the other party's back should only be sought in a true emergency — not just because you and your partner have had an argument. Restraining orders can have very serious consequences, such as keeping a person away from their home and prohibiting contact with their children. That is why courts require a high standard of proof in emergency motions, and judges expect applicants to give *all* of the details and circumstances giving rise to the motion. Far too often, judges make emergency restraining orders in reliance on the applicant's version of events, only to find later, when the other party's evidence is presented, that the applicant completely misled the court in order to get his/her spouse out of the matrimonial home or to get an advantage in the custody dispute. Beware: judges do not take kindly to being misled, and the consequences for abusing the court process or committing perjury can be severe and can damage a party's credibility for the duration of the court case.

In most jurisdictions, once the restraining order is made, the court will send it to the police for entry in their database. You should also deliver a certified copy of the order to your children's school if the order deals with the children in any way. Go to your local police station and speak to the officers about how best to protect yourself. Keep in mind that a restraining order is only a piece of paper, and that the police are not likely going to have the resources to assign a full-time officer to protect you. Until your ex-partner finds out about the order, he/she will not be aware of its terms, so you may not feel safe remaining in your home. Even after he/she learns of the order, he/she may be very angry, violently out of control, and unwilling to abide by it. The vast majority of ex-partners do comply with court orders and do not behave violently after separation. However, there is no denying that horribly tragic incidents of assault, abduction, and homicide have occurred despite restraining orders, bail orders, and probation orders prohibiting contact. Many victims of domestic violence do not have confidence that their ex-partners will comply with no-contact orders, so they move in with relatives or to shelters. If you feel that a restraining order is not sufficient to protect you, consult your lawyer and the police about what action you should take.

Should the court decide custody and access in every case where domestic violence has occurred?

In my opinion, the answer is no. While it is important to seek a restraining order in every case where domestic violence has occurred, I am not suggesting that every restraining order should be permanent. Just because a temporary restraining order has been issued, this does not necessarily mean that the parents will forever be required to deal with each other in a restricted way. I am also not suggesting that just because a restraining order has been issued, the parties must always and forever have a court decide their parenting issues. I believe it is important to draw a distinction between cases where there has been an ongoing pattern of violence or abuse, and cases where there was one isolated incident of relatively minor physical aggression (for example, a push or a shove) occurring at the very end of cohabitation.

The first category consists of couples whose relationships have been marked by long-standing victimization of one partner by the other throughout the relationship. Clearly a power imbalance and regime of fear and control exists, making it generally impossible for the parties to negotiate with each other as equal co-parents outside the court system — at least not until a great deal of supportive counselling for the victim and anger management therapy for the perpetrator have occurred and proven successful. And even then, the ex-partners may never be able to negotiate on an emotionally level playing field without the structure and security provided by the court system. Besides, in cases of long-standing abuse, the restraining order is probably going to be a permanent fixture in the parties' lives, making informal contact outside the realm of litigation legally impossible. So, for the unfortunate couples who fall within this category, it is entirely understandable and appropriate that they come to family court to resolve any parenting issues they may have (unless they can afford parenting coordinators), and this may well have to last throughout their children's entire childhoods.

The second category (when a single isolated incident of relatively minor physical aggression has occurred) is very different. I have seen thousands of couples whose relationships were not marked by any violence or abuse whatsoever until that one final argument or fight at the end of cohabitation, triggering the separation. Many couples stay together much longer than they should, living in extremely unhappy and stressful circumstances. Then one day an incident occurs — the proverbial "straw that breaks the camel's back" — and an all-out argument or fight erupts, resulting in one party pushing, shoving, or perhaps even slapping the other party. In this typical scenario, a temporary restraining order is made, and the court also decides temporary custody, access, and support. Then, over the next few months, the parties' tempers cool down, there are no recurrences of violence (there may or may not be an apology by the perpetrator), and the parties begin the process of letting go of their mutual anger and resentment. They are on the way to reinventing their relationship from ex-partners to co-parents. They may never be friends, but they have learned to be *friendly* and communicate civilly and in a "businesslike" way for the sake of their children. They put the past behind them and restrict their communications to the "business" of raising their children. They have the maturity and insight to understand that their children need them to make peace and co-operate with each other.

In my opinion, this category of couples (which comprises the majority of people I see) should not need family court involvement for long. Of course, it is important that the temporary restraining order and custody, access, and support orders be made to regulate conduct and provide security and structure during the first few months of separation. However, because the domestic violence here was an isolated incident as opposed to a regular aspect of the relationship, it is likely that once the parties have detached themselves from the emotional baggage surrounding their failed relationship (they may need counselling to achieve this), *and provided that no further incidents of violence or abuse have occurred,* there will eventually be no need for the restraining order. They should at that point be able to negotiate custody and access arrangements for their children without court intervention.

I am not for a moment suggesting that domestic violence or partner abuse, be it physical or emotional, be condoned or excused in any way. Domestic violence in any form, no matter how minor, is intolerable and unacceptable, and it has reached epidemic proportions. We all have a responsibility to prevent it and make it stop. Moreover, when children witness their parents arguing or fighting, this can constitute child abuse and may result in intervention by child protection authorities (see Chapter 11). However, I have learned over the years that no two situations are identical, and that labels such as "wife-beater," "victim," and "spouse abuser" can be simplistic and unhelpful. Most people lose their temper at least once in their lives and make mistakes, but they learn from those mistakes.

The existence of domestic violence is a relevant consideration in custody and access cases because it relates to a person's parenting skills. (For a discussion of the impact that domestic violence can have on the court's determination of a child's best interests, see Chapter 6.)

Substance abuse

If your ex-partner has an alcohol or drug problem and refuses to acknowledge it, you will probably have to go to family court to settle your custody and access arrangements. It is very difficult to negotiate these issues and put into place the kinds of protection your children need when the person you're negotiating with does not accept that he/she has a substance abuse problem or will not take steps to address it.

If your ex-partner denies the problem, you will have the onus of proving on a balance of probabilities that he/she has an alcohol or drug addiction. This can be challenging. If police or criminal records exist showing convictions for impaired driving or drug-related offences, you will want them produced. If your ex-partner has been disciplined or dismissed by an employer for substance abuse, you will want the employment records. If your ex-partner has previously attended a substance abuse treatment program, you will want a copy of the treatment facility's records to prove this. You may have photographs or videos to corroborate your allegations. You may be able to get affidavits from people who have observed your ex-partner using drugs or being intoxicated in the children's presence. You will need a lawyer to help you, as some of these documents are available only by court order, and the technical requirements for admissibility can be complicated.

If the court finds that a parent has a drug problem, it may order him/her to provide a hair sample drug screen analysis. Performed on a strand of hair, this test can detect a person's drug exposure over a specific period of several months (depending on the strand length) and the drug concentration (low, moderate, or high) in the hair. This evidence can indicate which drugs have been taken, how recently, and how extensively. In other words, a hair strand analysis can provide some idea of the seriousness and duration of the drug problem. In certain cases, hair strand tests have also been helpful in detecting alcoholism.

If a parent has been found to have a substance abuse problem, how will this impact his/her parenting rights? Obviously, the court's main concern is the safety and security of the children. They should not be left in the care of a person who is intoxicated or under the influence of mind-altering drugs, and they should not be exposed to illegal substances and drug paraphernalia. Some courts have the authority to order a parent to participate in a drug rehabilitation program and provide the other parent and the court with ongoing progress reports. In most cases, the court will impose safeguards to restrict the parent's access until such time as the judge is satisfied that the parent's problem is under control. For example, the court may order a parent to undergo urine testing several times a week and provide a hair strand analysis every six months in order to ensure that he/she is abstaining from alcohol and drugs. The access may have to be supervised by a responsible adult, usually a relative or friend selected by the parties. If they cannot agree on whom the supervisor should be, the judge will choose one of the people proposed by the parties. If there is no one willing to be present during visits, the access may have to occur in the presence of a paid access supervisor or at a community-operated supervised access centre, if you are fortunate enough to have one in your community.

If you or your ex-partner is struggling with a substance abuse problem, be mindful that your first priority must always be your children. Do not take risks with their safety and well-being. Every community has a child protection agency whose mandate is to ensure the protection and safety of children. These agencies are staffed with trained social workers who can provide guidance and support and make referrals for rehabilitation, counselling, and parenting education programs. If at any time you are questioning whether a parenting arrangement adequately protects your child, you should not hesitate to contact your local child protection agency.

Mental illness

When a parent has a serious personality disorder or other mental illness, it can be extremely difficult to negotiate reasonable parenting arrangements. A court action may be the only option. As you might expect, the proceeding will be much more complicated if the parent in question has not been diagnosed than if there is already an established diagnosis made by the person's doctor.

As you know, if you are alleging that your ex-partner has a mental health problem, you have the burden of proving this on a balance of probabilities. Where he/she has already been diagnosed by a doctor, you will want to present medical records or a letter from the doctor confirming the diagnosis and setting out the impact, if any, of the illness on the person's parenting capacity. Where there has been no diagnosis, you will need to convince a court, with the most reliable evidence possible, that your ex-partner's behaviour is suggestive of a mental health disorder. Affidavits from you, your relatives, friends, employers, neighbours, and community workers are often presented. You will probably be asking the court to order a psychiatric or psychological examination of your ex-partner. It should not surprise you to learn that you will need a lawyer to help you convince a court that this intrusion into your ex-partner's privacy is justified and necessary.

Sometimes it seems to me that every litigant I see believes the other party is mentally ill. Indeed, some people really do "lose it" when going through a separation, and maybe there is some form of "temporary madness" that comes into play during the highly stressful and traumatic final stages of a relationship. I have seen many cases in which an otherwise reasonable person did something bizarre and totally out of character during a breakup. In one case, a man took all of his wife's sweaters, washed them in hot water, and put them in the dryer so they shrank to the size of baby clothes. In another case, a woman showed up unexpectedly at her husband's office late one night to find him and his secretary stark naked in the throes of passion. She scooped up all of their clothes from the floor and promptly left. You can imagine the predicament that the husband and his secretary found themselves in! In another case, a woman ordered pizzas and Chinese food to be delivered to her husband's home in the middle of the night, every night for the first two weeks after the breakup. In yet another case, a husband changed the access code to his wife's telephone messaging system, preventing her from retrieving her messages for days. In all of these cases, the people involved were not mentally ill and quickly came to their senses with no further problems.

Breakups can be complicated and painful, and it is not unusual for each party to cast blame on the other, without considering his/her own degree of responsibility. Certainly it is not uncommon for depression to occur; probably most people appearing in family court would self-identify as being depressed. I believe this is a normal consequence of family breakdown. Many people attend counselling or therapy to help them cope with the grieving process that occurs when a family unit breaks down. This does not mean that they are mentally ill; on the contrary, it is a sign of maturity and insight when a person reaches out for help. The vast majority of these people are not mentally ill in a clinical sense, and pose no threat to their children. Be reasonable and fair, and think carefully before you run to court and tell the judge that your ex-partner is "crazy," "insane," or a "lunatic." Chances are that your ex-partner feels the same way about you, and if the two of you carry on as ridiculously as some couples I have seen in my courtroom, don't be surprised if the judge concludes that you're both "not all there"!

Mental illness is not a weapon in a parent's arsenal to try to embarrass the other parent, or to delay or complicate a court case, or to alienate the other parent from his/her children. Identifying someone as being mentally ill is a serious accusation. Your own credibility, integrity, and judgment will be called into question if it turns out you have unfairly denigrated your ex-partner to further your own agenda. Any parent who would do this is not focusing on his/her children's best interests, and this is not likely to be overlooked by the judge. So before you decide to ask a court to deny or restrict your ex-partner's access to his/her children by reason of mental illness, ask a lawyer to review your evidence and tell you whether it is likely to meet the evidentiary onus imposed on you by the law. If you are wondering whether your ex-partner's conduct may be harmful to your child, you should call your local child protection agency for assistance.

If the judge makes a finding that a parent has a mental health problem, the question to be decided will be the extent, if any, to which the mental health problem impacts upon the parent's ability to provide proper care for the child. This is where a psychiatric or psychological report can be very helpful, as judges are not doctors and have to rely on the expert opinions and recommendations of qualified mental health professionals. The report will indicate the nature of the parent's disability (symptoms and diagnosis), the impact of the disorder on daily functioning and especially parenting duties, the preferred treatment (medication and/or therapy), the patient's level of insight and acceptance of the diagnosis, and the patient's degree of compliance with the treatment regime.

In my experience, many people with mental health disabilities are highly motivated and wonderful parents, and provided they follow their doctors' treatment directions (medication and/or therapy), their mental health issues are largely irrelevant. It is rare that a parent's mental illness interferes with a normal parent-child relationship.

When the court finds that a child may be at risk because of a parent's mental health problem, this is almost always because the parent refuses to acknowledge the problem, or refuses to get help, or to consistently follow the treatment plan as directed by the doctor. In such cases, the court may impose the same kinds of access restrictions as described above in the section dealing with substance abuse. Access will be completely denied to a mentally ill parent only if the risk to the child of physical or emotional harm caused by the parent's behaviour is so great that no restrictions or conditions could adequately protect the child.

Child abuse or neglect

Every jurisdiction has laws protecting the safety of children, and every community has a child protection agency. Chapter 11 explains how and why a private custody dispute between parents can become the subject of state intervention by child protection authorities. However, for the purposes of this section, my point is that when one parent accuses the other of committing child abuse or neglect, it is almost impossible to negotiate a mutually agreeable custody and access plan because such accusations are very inflammatory and rarely admitted to. Parents in this situation almost always require a judge to determine their parental rights.

Quite apart from the legal definitions of *abuse* and *neglect,* which vary depending on the laws where you live, I have found that most people apply wildly subjective, self-serving, and divergent definitions of these terms. Some people think that it is abusive or neglectful to allow a child to watch certain television shows, play with certain toys, listen to certain types of music, eat certain foods, or associate with certain kinds of people. Litigants in family court routinely toss the words "abuse" and "neglect" at each other like volleyballs. You are well advised to consult a lawyer and your local child protection agency before hurling an accusation of child abuse or neglect against your ex-partner. Remember that if you have exaggerated the facts and the court disagrees with your labelling of the other parent as abusive or neglectful, you will be sending a clear message to the judge that you are being unfair to the other parent. This will not stand you in good stead when your own credibility, reasonableness, and parenting skills are assessed. Keep in mind that part of being a good parent is the ability to foster a good relationship between the child and the other parent.

As you know, you will bear the burden of establishing on a balance of probabilities that your ex-partner committed the misconduct you are complaining about. If the misconduct in question constitutes a criminal offence such as assault or sexual assault, then the police should also be involved and charges may be laid. (The interrelationship between family court and criminal court is discussed in Chapter 10.)

---

1   In jurisdictions where same-sex partners are not entitled to the same rights as opposite-sex partners, restraining orders may not be available in family court, and the criminal court system may have to be accessed.

CHAPTER FOUR

ALTERNATIVES TO LITIGATION

IF NONE OF THE EXCEPTIONS SET OUT IN THE LAST CHAPTER APPLY TO YOU, THEN YOU AND YOUR EX-PARTNER SHOULD CONSIDER ONE OF THE FOLLOWING ALTERNATIVES TO STARTING A COURT CASE. The reason is simple: when you start a court case, you are starting a war. When you choose one of the following methods of resolving your case, known as *alternative dispute resolution*, you are making peace. With one exception *(arbitration)*, these alternatives allow you and your ex-partner to retain the decision-making powers rather than give them up to a judge. This increases your chances of being satisfied with the results. I also firmly believe that these less argumentative methods of problem solving help reduce conflict and promote mature behaviour through rational discussion.

Mediation

The most common alternative to litigation is mediation.[1] A mediator is an impartial professional with expertise in helping parties negotiate fair, constructive, and mutually agreeable resolutions to their disputes. Mediation is time-effective and inexpensive compared to litigation. It is such a successful method of dispute resolution that it is widely used to settle disputes in labour law, the commercial sector, and most kinds of civil lawsuits. Most family mediators who deal with custody and access disputes are mental health professionals such as psychologists and social workers. Most family mediators who deal mainly with financial and property issues are lawyers who have had extensive training and certification in mediation. Some mediators are cross-trained and have degrees in both law and social work.

A mediator's job, as a neutral third party, is to help the parents define the issues in dispute and explore a variety of options that take into account the children's specific needs, with a view to achieving consensus. The goal is to reach a fair and workable agreement with individualized solutions that satisfy the underlying interests of both parents and each of their children. The mediator may meet with each parent separately to begin with, and then will meet with both parents as many times as necessary to resolve the dispute. Lawyers generally do not go to mediation with the parties, but they should review any agreement reached before it is signed, to ensure the parties get independent legal advice before committing themselves.

Here are some typical issues mediators can help parents resolve:

- How will major decisions such as living arrangements, education, healthcare, religious training, and extra-curricular activities be made?
- When will the children be with each parent?
- How will the visitation schedule be adjusted if lateness or cancellation occurs?
- How will the parents communicate with each other about the children (phone, writing in a communication log, e-mail, and so on)?
- How will birthdays, religious holidays, school vacation periods, and other special occasions be handled?
- What role will relatives play in the children's lives?
- How will any future disputes be resolved?

Parents can also use mediation to resolve financial and matrimonial property issues. In fact, any dispute can be mediated.

Rather than take sides or make decisions for you, the mediator helps you resolve misunderstandings and communicate with each other more clearly by reducing hostilities and competitive feelings. The mediator guides the communication process so that everyone has a chance to be heard. Various options are explored so that the best possible solution can be reached. The mediator may offer suggestions, but the final agreement is up to you and your ex-partner.

While mediation is not therapy, it can be therapeutic because it helps parents in several ways. It allows the parents themselves to decide and discuss what is important to them. It encourages a co-operative spirit rather than an adversarial one. It inspires parents to be creative and to devise parenting plans that meet the unique needs of the entire family.

Mediation may not resolve all the issues, but even partial agreements can help to limit the time, expense and uncertainty of going to court. For example, the parties may have been able to agree on custody and child support but not on access. In the rare case when mediation has not been successful in resolving the dispute, the parties can resort to the court system and have a judge decide the issue. Sometimes the parties will agree in advance that if the dispute is not resolved, the mediator will write a report explaining to the judge why the parties were not able to agree. This is called *open mediation*. Some couples prefer *closed mediation,* which means that the mediator will not disclose to the judge what the parties said during the mediation and will not explain why the parties failed to agree.

Many courts located in large cities and towns throughout North America have on-site staff mediators who provide free services with a view to diverting families away from the costly, time-consuming, and stressful route of litigation. Some courts do not require parents to launch a court case in order to avail themselves of the mediation service. Even if you are required to begin a court case, you can ask for a referral to mediation instead of or before seeing a judge. In fact, in some courts, *every* case is screened to determine the parties' eligibility for mediation, without the need for a party to ask.

If the family court in your area does not offer free mediation services, you should still inquire about the possibility of mediation from the court office or your local child protection agency, and of course you should always discuss this with your lawyer. Most communities have a number of family service associations that can refer parents to affordable mediation services. You may also wish to contact Family Mediation Canada (www.fmc.ca). In the United States contact the Association for Conflict Resolution (www.acrnet.org/about/CR-FAQ.htm#find) or the Academy of Family Mediators (www.mediate.com/index.cfm). These organizations can give you a great deal of information about mediation and help you find certified family mediators in your area.

Although mediation is an extremely successful method of dispute resolution, it is not appropriate for everyone, particularly in cases where there has been violence or abuse. When one party is afraid of or intimidated by his/her ex-partner, mediation may not be desirable. Family mediators conduct a screening process when they meet a couple to assess whether mediation is suitable for them. The mediator will consider the following:

1) whether both parents are motivated to try to settle the dispute;
2) whether both parents are capable of stating their needs and interests;
3) whether both parents understand their rights and responsibilities under the law;
4) whether both parents are consenting to participate in the mediation process; and
5) whether a power imbalance exists within the couple by reason of fear or intimidation that would make it impossible for one parent to negotiate with the other as an equal.

If your case has been accepted for mediation by a qualified family mediator, approach the experience with an open mind and an open heart. Consider it not only as a way to resolve your disputes but also as a learning experience. Try to forge a new way of communicating with your ex-partner, using the techniques applied in the mediation sessions. You have nothing to lose and everything to gain, but remember: don't sign any agreement without getting thorough advice from your lawyer.

Collaborative law

One of the newest and most exciting developments gaining momentum in the family law field is collaborative law. Collaborative lawyers have training similar to mediators and work with their clients and one another in a non-confrontational way to negotiate comprehensive settlements of family disputes without going to court. In fact, it is a basic requirement of the collaborative family law process that the parties do not go to court. The parties and lawyers must sign a contract specifically stating that if they are unable to reach an agreement (which almost never happens), the lawyers and any other professionals retained in the process must resign: they are disqualified from participating in any litigation related to the dispute. In the unlikely event that the parties are unable to settle the dispute and court action is necessary, the parties would have to retain different lawyers from the ones they hired in the collaborative process.

The collaborative process differs from mediation in several important ways:

1) In mediation, the parents meet with a neutral third party (a mediator) who assists them to negotiate a mutually acceptable resolution. However, in the collaborative process, there is usually no mediator because the parties' lawyers have the necessary negotiation skills. However, there is always the option of including a mediator if everyone feels it would be helpful. This is called *collaborative mediation.*

2) In mediation, the parties' lawyers rarely participate directly in the process. They act more as coaches, and get involved only when an agreement has been reached, and their primary role is to advise the parties of their legal rights before they sign the agreement. In the collaborative process, the lawyers are essential, as they take a lead role in the negotiations.

3) Mediation can occur during or before a family court proceeding, whereas in the collaborative process the lawyers and parties sign a contract agreeing not to go to court.

In the collaborative family law process, the parents and their lawyers work together as members of a settlement team, rather than working against each other as opposing parties. Although collaborative lawyers protect their clients' legal interests and are bound by the same confidentiality rules as other lawyers, they work co-operatively with opposing parties and their lawyers in a process of principled negotiation. The parents learn to focus on their common interests, understand each other's perspectives and concerns, exchange information, treat each other with respect, and explore the widest possible range of choices. The goal is co-operation, not confrontation, and parents are taught to let go of the past in order to focus on the future. Because litigation is not an option, it can never be threatened and neither parent is permitted to take advantage of the other. Collaborative lawyers insist that parents act ethically and in good faith at all times;

they must be honest and co-operate fully with each other in sharing information, particularly regarding financial and property issues.

The collaborative process works mostly through face-to-face negotiations with both parents and their lawyers present. These are called *four-way meetings*. An agenda is agreed upon, timetables are set regarding the sharing of financial information, and sometimes other professionals are involved, such as property valuators, pension experts, financial planners, parenting coaches, and child psychologists. The lawyers represent their clients' interests but also listen to the other party's concerns with a view to achieving compromise.

There is no question that parents who retain collaborative family lawyers can resolve their disputes more quickly and inexpensively than those who resort to litigation. One big cost-saving feature is that instead of each party retaining his/her own expert (for example, a property valuator), the parties agree to jointly hire one expert and to be bound by that person's opinion. The expert can even be part of the negotiation process by joining the meetings and guiding part of the discussion.

As the collaborative law process does not involve litigation, parents do not surrender their decision-making authority to a stranger. They are engaged in creative problem solving rather than assigning blame and seeking revenge. In addition, many people prefer the collaborative process because it allows them to maintain their privacy; the financial and personal details of their family breakdown are not accessible to the public in court files.

In short, parents who have the maturity to appreciate that it is in their children's best interests that decisions be made in an atmosphere of mutual respect, dignity, and co-operation should explore the collaborative family law process. To learn more, consult Collaborative Family Lawyers of Canada (www.collaborativelaw.ca), International Academy of Collaborative Professionals (www.collaborativepractice.com), Resolution (www.resolution.org.uk), and the Collaborative Family Law Group (www.collablaw.org.uk).

As with mediation, collaborative law is not for everyone. The process requires parents to have at least some maturity in attitude and perspective, and they must have the ability and willingness to listen to each other's views and communicate calmly and respectfully. In addition, in the unlikely event that the negotiations fall apart (for example, if a party is acting in bad faith) and it becomes necessary to go to court, the parties have to hire new lawyers. This can be more expensive than if a court case had been started in the first place. If you are not sure whether you and your ex-partner would be good candidates for the collaborative process, you should speak to a collaborative family lawyer.

Arbitration

If neither mediation nor the collaborative process appeals to you, and if you prefer to have a third party decide the issues, the option of arbitration is available in many jurisdictions. In arbitration, both parties submit their evidence and arguments to a third-party decision maker (an arbitrator) whom they (or more accurately, their lawyers) have agreed to hire. Because arbitrations occur outside the court system, the parties maintain their privacy, as there is no publicly accessible court file containing personal information. The obvious advantage in choosing the arbitrator is the certainty that the decision will be made by someone in whom you both have confidence, presumably because that person has the necessary knowledge and expertise to render the best possible decision.

There are three reasons why some people find arbitration appealing: (1) all decisions in the case will be made by one decision maker; (2) the decision maker is a family law specialist; and (3) the timetable is set by the parties and does not depend on court schedules, so the process is faster than using the court system. These are important features not always guaranteed in family court.

In the court system, litigants do not get to select their judge; cases are randomly assigned to judges. There can be great unpredictability in the court system because in some courts there is no *single-judge case management system,* meaning that the parties see a different judge each time they come to court. When there is no single judge responsible for the case from beginning to end, much time and effort is spent bringing each judge handling the case up to speed, and there is a risk that different judges may reach inconsistent conclusions. It can be difficult to make progress and achieve settlements, since no one judge ever becomes sufficiently familiar with the parties and their circumstances on an ongoing basis. If the family court in your area does not have a single-judge case management system, you may wish to talk with your lawyer about arbitration as a way of ensuring that you have only one decision maker resolving your issues.

Quite apart from the problems that can arise when multiple judges handle the same case, there are some courts in which judges are "generalists" and do not specialize in family law. A generalist judge has expertise in a variety of areas and hears many different types of cases besides family law, such as criminal law, medical malpractice, labour law, bankruptcy law, and commercial litigation. Some people believe that family law adjudication requires specialized expertise and sensitivity because of the unique dynamic between litigant family members, the importance of the decisions being made, and the impact of those decisions on the lives of parents and children whose relationships will continue long after the court case is over. Many family law lawyers feel strongly that family law cases should be heard only by "specialist" judges who spend most, if not all, of their time in family court. It is thought that judges who specialize in family law are the best equipped to resolve family law disputes because of their training and experience not only in family law but in conducting case conferences (meetings to define, discuss, and resolve issues) and settlement conferences (defined below) in a child-focused way. If you live in an area where generalist judges hear family court cases, and if your lawyer thinks that this can be problematic, then you may wish to consider having your family law dispute decided by an arbitrator who is a family law specialist.

Parties who choose arbitration almost always have lawyers, and the arbitrator will invariably be a leading family law lawyer. The evidence will be presented much like in a regular court case, although the parties may inject some flexibility into the procedure. The arbitrator will decide the disputed issues much like a judge would. The parties will be bound by the arbitrator's decision in the same way as if the decision had been made by a court. The parties can also agree in advance that any minor post-decision disputes (for example, disagreements over vacation time) will be decided by the arbitrator — sometimes even by telephone conference call. Most jurisdictions have legislation governing arbitrations to ensure that arbitrators are properly trained and that the basic principles of due process applicable in a court of law are applied. Some jurisdictions even require that all family law arbitration decisions be registered with the government.

As you might expect, there can be downsides to arbitration:

1) It can be expensive because the arbitrator will charge an hourly rate that in most cases will be as much as that charged by a first-rate lawyer. Usually the parties share the cost of the arbitrator equally, although if there is great disparity in the parties' incomes, they may agree to divide the arbitrator's fees in accordance with the proportionate difference in their incomes. Sometimes the arbitrator will decide how his/her fees are to be apportioned between the parties, in addition to any costs awards that may be made in the same way that a judge might order costs at the end of a court case.

2) Once an arbitrator has been agreed to, the parties must remain committed to that person and will be bound by his/her decision unless they agree to switch arbitrators. A party who doesn't like the way things are going with the arbitrator cannot easily get the case away from him/her. This is a big difference from litigation. In a court case, the parties are usually sure to have at least two different judges handling their case if they go to trial. This is because in most jurisdictions, the trial judge will probably not be the same judge who made the temporary orders in the case. A party who didn't like the approach taken by the judge who made the temporary orders will have a different judge hearing the trial. In arbitration, there is no easy way to get the case before a different decision maker.

3) Once the arbitrator's decision has been made, it will probably still be necessary to go to court to enforce the decision. There is some risk at that point that a party will try to challenge or appeal the decision, but this is rarely done. After all, what is the point of jointly deciding on a decision maker and paying that person to conduct a hearing and make a decision if you aren't prepared to accept the decision as final?

I believe that parents wishing to have their disputes resolved by a third party should not have to incur the expense of paying a private decision maker. Taxpayers already pay a lot of money to fund family courts, which were created to provide decision-making services by highly qualified, independent, and impartial judges. That being said, it must be acknowledged that in communities plagued by court backlogs, or where single-judge case management by family law "specialist" judges is unavailable, arbitration is a very attractive alternative to court litigation. You should consider arbitration only if your lawyer and your ex-partner's lawyer agree that this is the best route.

Mediation-Arbitration

Another option you should consider (if the law where you live allows it) is a very popular one because it combines the best features of mediation and arbitration. The parties proceed with mediation, but they agree in advance that if they are unable to reach agreement on any issue, the mediator will become an arbitrator and decide the issue. The major advantage of this mechanism is its efficiency: if the mediation fails, it is not necessary to go to court or hire an arbitrator. The person making the decision will already be familiar with all of the details and can quickly make a well-informed decision.

In practice, it is rarely necessary for a mediator-arbitrator to stop the mediation and conduct an arbitration. This is because the parties have a strong incentive to reach an agreement. They know from the outset that the mediator-arbitrator will decide the issue if a mediated solution cannot be reached, so they tend to conduct themselves reasonably and courteously. No one wants to make a bad impression in front of a decision maker who is going to remember everything that has been said during the process.

In addition, the parties at a mediation-arbitration are highly motivated to listen to and apply the mediator-arbitrator's input and proposed solutions, since it is likely that if the parties cannot agree, the mediator-arbitrator's suggestions will become the final decision. For example, Parent A argues that the child should attend public school, and Parent B feels that the child should attend private school. As part of the mediation process, the mediator-arbitrator will delve beneath the parties' stated demands to understand *why* each parent feels that his/her choice of school would be best for the child. Parent A may be concerned about the cost of private school, and Parent B may be motivated by a belief that private schools offer superior education to public schools. The mediator-arbitrator will help the parties work co-operatively to find the best solution to meet each parent's interests, such as seeking a private school that offers subsidies; or finding a public school that offers many of the same education programs as a private school; or agreeing to reduce other expenses to make the private school fees more affordable; or agreeing to send the child to a private school for a specific period of time; or they might agree to send the child to a public school and supplement the child's education with additional tutoring and programs.

Assume that the mediator-arbitrator has expressed a strong preference for one of the above options. If the parents are unable to agree on a solution, it is highly likely that the mediator-arbitrator will decide in favour of the option he/she recommended. So why bother paying a mediator-arbitrator to conduct an arbitration hearing, plus additional fees to your own lawyer, if you already know the outcome?

One big difference between mediation and mediation-arbitration is the role lawyers play. In mediation, the parties' lawyers usually participate only at the final stage, when an agreement has been reached; they give the parties legal advice before signing the written agreement. However, in mediation-arbitration, the parties' lawyers usually participate throughout the process. This is because there is the possibility that an agreement may not be reached, and the lawyers need to know everything that has happened so they can properly represent their clients in the arbitration hearing. Consequently, mediation-arbitration may be a more expensive option than mediation due to the legal fees incurred. However, when you factor in the convenience of having the mediation and the decision provided by the same person, it is probably more cost-effective to pay the legal fees for one procedure, rather than have to commence litigation or arbitration and rehash all of the issues before a different decision maker (a judge or an arbitrator) if the mediation is unsuccessful.

---

1   Phillip Epstein, a prominent Canadian family law lawyer, estimates that 60 per cent of divorcing couples in Canada opt for mediation: *Toronto Star*, January 14, 2008, p. A-1.

CHAPTER FIVE

LAWYERS:
WHY YOU NEED ONE, HOW TO CHOOSE ONE, AND HOW TO MEASURE PERFORMANCE

THE MOST FREQUENTLY ASKED QUESTION I HEAR FROM LITIGANTS IS, DO I NEED A LAWYER? The answer is a definite YES. Any judge or lawyer will tell you that a case is likely to be more complicated, stressful, and time-consuming when one party (or both) is unrepresented than if both parties have legal counsel. In this chapter, I will explain why it is essential that every person going through a separation, divorce, or any form of negotiations with an ex-partner should have a lawyer (or, at the very least, access to legal advice), especially if they will be going to court. I will also give you some tips on how to find a lawyer and how to measure your lawyer's performance.

Litigants without lawyers
There are two categories of litigants who appear in court without lawyers: unrepresented litigants and self-represented litigants. An *unrepresented litigant* is a person who wants to have a lawyer but cannot afford one.[1] A *self-represented litigant* is a person who can afford a lawyer but believes that he/she does not need one. My primary objective in writing this chapter is to persuade self-represented litigants to reconsider that belief.

In the last decade, there has been a tremendous increase in the number of litigants without lawyers appearing in family courts throughout North America. Although many courts do not keep reliable statistics, studies conducted in Canada and the United States indicate that the percentage of family court litigants without lawyers ranges from 20 to 70 per cent.[2] The impact of these people on the justice system has been overwhelming because the system was not designed to be navigated by people without knowledge of the law or the procedure. Many lawyers and judges consider the growing phenomenon of unrepresented and self-represented litigants to be the most serious problem facing the court system today.[3] Litigants without lawyers frequently create chaos, frustration, and delay. They make the work of a family court judge extremely challenging. They complicate the lives of family law lawyers to such an extent that many lawyers will refuse to take a case if the other party is representing him/herself.

Unrepresented litigants
Most family law lawyers charge anywhere from $200 to $500 per hour, and many lawyers will not agree to take a case without a deposit (called a *retainer*) of at least several thousand dollars, depending on the complexity of the case and the number of issues in dispute. People who have recently separated are usually experiencing significant financial strain because the same amount of money that was maintaining one household must now maintain two households. Often there are moving expenses, and sometimes new furniture and vehicles must be purchased, as the parties adjust to their new lives as single parents. The period immediately following separation is not likely to be a time when parents have extra funds available for legal fees. Consequently it is no surprise that so many family court litigants who sincerely want legal representation are genuinely unable to afford it.

Although most jurisdictions have government-funded legal aid programs, eligibility for legal aid is usually reserved for people whose incomes fall below the poverty line. Unfortunately there are many people whose incomes are too high to qualify for legal aid but are too low to afford a lawyer. These people are often left no choice but to proceed without a lawyer, and in my view this is a serious social problem that undermines every citizen's fundamental right to access the justice system. Without access to justice, there may be no justice. It is incumbent on everyone who works in the family justice system — lawmakers, judges, the legal profession, and social service organizations —

to find solutions to this dilemma. Parents in crisis must have access to affordable legal representation so their conflicts can be resolved expeditiously, fairly, and in the best interests of their children.

If you have been denied legal aid and do not have the money to retain a lawyer, you should at the very least try to raise enough money for a consultation with a lawyer. In those few hours, the lawyer will be able to explain your rights and tell you what evidence you will need to respond to your ex-partner's claim and/or make a claim of your own (custody, access, support, and so on). If you have prepared court documents on your own, take them to a lawyer to ensure they are complete and that they include all of the claims you can put forth. Believe me, this will be money well spent. You cannot imagine how many litigants without lawyers have their claims rejected because their documentation is deficient.

Of course, even if you have managed to pay for a legal consultation, you will still be on your own in the courtroom if you are unrepresented. You should find out if any free or reduced-fee legal assistance is available in your community: inquire at the legal aid office, ask the family court staff, call your local lawyers' association, and contact the social service agencies in your community that offer assistance to people who have experienced family breakdown. Some university law faculties run free legal aid clinics staffed by law students. Some lawyers' associations maintain lists of lawyers who represent a limited number of clients on a voluntary basis (called *pro bono* services). Many family courts have legal aid lawyers on duty (called *duty counsel*) who provide free legal advice and limited in-court assistance for unrepresented litigants. Obviously there is not much that a lawyer can do for you if he/she meets you only a few minutes before you enter the courtroom, but it is still worthwhile to get as much legal advice and assistance as you possibly can.

Self-represented litigants: family court is not like TV

It has never ceased to amaze me that so many people honestly believe they do not need a lawyer, even though they have no legal training or court experience whatsoever. At least several times a week I am told by self-represented litigants that they regularly watch *Judge Judy* or some other law-related television program, which in their view has more than adequately prepared them for their court cases! And just as often,

I am told by equally confident litigants that they feel totally equipped to represent themselves in court because they have consulted a self-help Web site. These people are usually in for a rude awakening in the form of a major reality check when they get to court.

Family court does not work like a television show. On *Judge Judy,* each party tells the judge his/her story, and then the judge makes a decision, and this all happens in a few minutes; it *has* to, because they have to fit two cases plus commercials into a thirty-minute show! Remember that *Judge Judy* is *not* a family law show dealing with child custody or the division of matrimonial property; it is a small claims court television show resolving minor damage claims. It should be obvious to any reasonable person that judicial decisions dealing with the consequences of family breakdown cannot be made in the same way as the simple contractual disputes on television court programs. And yet every day people come to my court saying, "Judge, can you hurry up and make a decision as I'm double-parked and I have to get back to work in an hour!" I feel like responding, "One custody decision coming up! Would you like fries with that?"

As you know from Chapter 2, most family court decisions are made in *motions,* which are based on *written* evidence (called *affidavits*), not oral testimony. You cannot just come to court and tell the judge your story and get a rapid decision. Now you may be thinking, "So what's the big deal? Instead of telling the judge my story verbally, I'll just write it down. I don't need a lawyer to do that. No one knows my story better than me." It's not that simple.

Evidence must be relevant

Only information that is *relevant* to the issues in dispute will be admissible in court. You need a lawyer to help you decide what aspects of your story are relevant, because legal relevance is a difficult concept for many people to understand. Family court judges are regularly presented with affidavits full of irrelevant information and accusations. These things only serve to inflame the parties' hostilities and do nothing to help us make our decisions.

For example, in custody cases, the issue before the court is "What living arrangement and parenting plan would be in the child's best interests?" Parents should be focusing on the child's needs, their parenting skills, and their respective plans to care for the child in the future. Judges need to know a great deal of information: how the child-care responsibilities were divided before the parents separated (if they lived together); whether the child is more emotionally bonded to one parent than the other; the child's routines and the parents' work schedules; the parents' living arrangements; how the child's schooling and extracurricular activities will be affected by each parent's custody proposal; how each parent plans to work co-operatively with the other parent to ensure that the effect of the separation on the child is minimized. These are only a few of the questions judges need answered in custody cases. (For a complete discussion of the factors considered in custody disputes, see Chapter 6.)

Unfortunately, very few self-represented litigants give the court *relevant* information. I constantly read affidavits from hurt and angry parents bitterly detailing each other's sexual infidelities. Many self-represented parents want to focus on the fact that their ex-partner left them for someone else, and their affidavits concentrate exclusively on the personality flaws of the other parent's new partner (whom, in some cases, they have never met!). I have seen affidavits in which the entire dispute revolved around the parents' relationships with their in-laws, or their financial problems, or their disputes over religion. I even had one custody case in which the parents focused only on each other's bad cooking! It is astounding that so many affidavits in custody cases make absolutely no mention of the child! Imagine how frustrating this can be for a judge trying to obtain the necessary *relevant* information in order to make the best possible decision for the child.

Ironically, a great many self-represented parents believe that by bad-mouthing their ex-partners, they are improving their own chances of getting custody. They do not realize that this may very well have the opposite effect. When a person concentrates only on irrelevant mudslinging, it usually tells the judge much more about the mudslinger than about the person being criticized.

Judges are not private detectives or investigators; we must rely on the litigants to provide the evidence upon which we base our decisions. Self-represented parents who give the court nothing but irrelevant information are in for a surprise when the judge tells them to come back in a few weeks (or months if the court is backlogged) with the *relevant* information that is required for the court to do its job. This could be avoided if you have a lawyer.

Evidence must be admissible

You also need a lawyer to make sure your story is being told in a way that follows the rules of evidence. One of the most important of these rules is the *hearsay rule,* which prohibits a person from quoting something that another person has said if the purpose of putting that quote into evidence is to have the court accept the quote as being true. For example, you are not allowed to put into evidence "My neighbour Sally told me that she saw my ex-partner hitting the child" and expect the judge to accept this as proof that your ex-partner hit the child. You would have to provide an affidavit from Sally herself, or if it were a trial, Sally would have to testify. The information must come directly from Sally, not second-hand through you, so that she can be cross-examined by your ex-partner's lawyer. That is the only way for the judge to test Sally's credibility and decide whether to believe that your ex-partner hit the child.

The hearsay rule is very complicated because it contains a myriad of variations and exceptions. Law students spend months learning about this rule; it is a minefield for the untrained. In my experience, the hearsay rule is the biggest pitfall that self-represented litigants encounter. It is natural to want to give the court important information you have received from other people such as doctors, teachers, police officers, friends, and relatives. This information can only be presented to the court in the proper way, and the hearsay rule must be applied correctly. Frequently, self-represented people are shocked to find that the most crucial information they were planning to rely on in their court case was ruled inadmissible because it violated the hearsay rule. This frustration and disappointment could have been avoided if a lawyer had been consulted.

You also need a lawyer to tell you what evidence you will need to prove your claim and to make sure that your proof (such as business records, police records, letters from doctors and schools, photographs, and videos) is legally admissible. If your case involves a division of matrimonial property or a claim for child or spousal support, you will need to compile a detailed financial statement and attach income tax documents and possibly other proof of income (called *financial disclosure*). If you are self-employed, a number of business financial records (possibly including mortgage and car loan applications, and bank and credit card statements) will likely need to be produced. Without the help of a lawyer, it will be difficult to know what documents you will need, or what documents to ask for if the other party is self-employed. If you do not produce the necessary documents, the judge may have to adjourn the case to another date and you may be ordered to pay the other party's legal costs stemming from the wasted court appearance. Or even worse, the judge may decide to proceed with the case even though you are missing some documents, and the court may draw a negative inference from your failure to fully disclose your financial circumstances. Believe me: if this happens, you are not likely to be happy with the result. If you can afford a lawyer (and most people can afford at least a consultation), why take the risk of having improper evidence rejected by the court? Why take the risk that a court may make a decision based on incomplete evidence?

Substantive and procedural law

The law has two components: substantive law and procedural law. In family law, the *substantive law* tells us what our actual rights and obligations are, such as entitlement to a divorce, division of matrimonial property, or custody, access, and child and spousal support. Most people do not know the law and are not fully aware of their legal rights and obligations. You need a lawyer to review your situation and advise you of your legal rights and obligations. No book, Web site, or television show can substitute for individual advice and representation from a family law lawyer. Every day you will find self-represented litigants in family court making claims they are not entitled to make. For example, I have had people ask me for custody of their pets or to deport their ex-partners (some of whom are citizens!). I have been asked to make orders governing what the other parent will put in his/her will. I have had people ask me to make orders transferring assets that do not belong to either party or to overturn the decisions of other judges even though I am not an appeal judge. I have had people apply for custody of children who reside in other countries. I even had one case in which a parent asked me to order the other parent not to have any more children! It is important to understand the seriousness of commencing a court case. It should only be done on a lawyer's advice, so that you can be sure you are making a proper legal claim and are going to the correct court. Remember, if you sue someone and lose, you can expect to pay the other party's legal costs. Judges have little sympathy for self-represented people who haul their ex-partners into court and seek remedies the court has no authority to grant.

Quite apart from knowing the substantive law, you also need to be aware of the *procedural law,* which contains all of the rules governing how court cases are run. There are forms to be filled out, time limits to abide by, notices to be given to the other party, records to keep, and a multitude of other procedures to follow. In addition, not every family court has the authority to deal with every aspect of family disputes. In some jurisdictions, there are two types of family courts: one dealing with custody, access, and support; and another dealing with divorce and matrimonial property. In some jurisdictions married couples might be treated differently than unmarried couples. In some jurisdictions same-sex couples might be treated differently than opposite-sex couples.

If you represent yourself and go to the wrong court or fail to follow the proper procedures, you will not only suffer frustration and confusion but will also run the risk of having your case dismissed. At the very least, you will endure delays, as your case will probably have to be postponed over and over again until you get it right. Think of all the time from work that you will have to miss or babysitters you will have to hire due to wasted court appearances. Think of the costs you may be ordered to pay to the other party if your failure to follow proper procedures requires the case to be postponed. Imagine going to so much effort and then getting no results. All of this can be avoided if you hire a lawyer. Your lawyer will know which court to go to, and he/she will follow all of the procedures to make the court case proceed smoothly. Self-represented people cannot possibly know what to do without a great deal of training or assistance. You are urged to retain a lawyer to manage your case.

The "objectivity" factor

So far we have looked at the problems arising for self-represented litigants due to a lack of knowledge and legal training. There is another equally important reason why you should never represent yourself in family court. There is a famous expression that says, "A lawyer who represents himself has a fool for a client." Truer words were never spoken. Even if you have the necessary legal knowledge, you should not represent yourself in a dispute with your ex-partner because you cannot be objective about yourself, your ex-partner, or your children.

No one expects recently separated parents to view their situations objectively, at least not during the emotionally fragile period when parents are negotiating a resolution to their parenting and financial issues. For example, very few parents I see in my courtroom are able to tell me one positive thing about their ex-partners. And yet, these are people who loved each other at one time (and, in some cases, for many years). We all know that no one is all good or all bad and that both parents must have had some positive attributes that drew them together. Unfortunately, at the time of separation (and for some time afterwards, depending on their maturity levels), most parents are unable to remember or appreciate each other's good qualities. Virtually every litigant I see views him/herself as a victim; rarely does anyone feel that he/she bears any responsibility whatsoever for the breakup. Of course, family court judges know that the most important *victims* in a family breakdown are the children, who did nothing to cause the separation and did not choose to have two parents who hate each other.

When dealing with an ex-partner, especially right after a breakup, too many emotions can get in the way to allow a parent to dispassionately assess his/her own parenting plan and that of the other parent. Parents in this situation are generally so immersed in their own hurt and anger that they cannot take a step back and see the other parent's point of view or the children's perspectives. Counsellors and therapists can help parents heal emotionally so they can reinvent their relationship from ex-partners to co-parents. Equally importantly, parents need family law lawyers to help identify the issues and realistically appraise the circumstances so they can make the best and most appropriate decisions for themselves and their children. A family law lawyer is the only person qualified to tell you not only what your rights are but also whether you should be using the court system rather than one of the alternative methods of dispute resolution discussed in Chapter 4.

If you decide to go to court, a lawyer is the only person qualified to guide you through that process efficiently and productively. In court, the lawyer will make professional, child-focused, settlement-oriented submissions on your behalf. This is infinitely better than having litigants spout off in front of the judge in an emotionally immature way, which so often happens with self-represented litigants who cannot contain their anger in the heat of the moment. I cannot tell you how many times I have seen self-represented litigants, who have been accused of having bad tempers and poor impulse control, throw huge tantrums in court while denying the existence of an anger management problem! If this is how they behave in front of a judge, when they should be on their best behaviour, I wonder how they treat other people. Self-represented litigants shoot themselves in the foot all the time because they are too emotionally distraught to present themselves in a positive light when advocating in court. It should be obvious that negotiations between two people who are angry with each other will be much more effective and successful if they are conducted professionally by lawyers rather than by the parties directly.

Only a lawyer can give you the all-important advice you need to make a sound settlement proposal and to assess offers received from the other party. You need a lawyer to conduct effective settlement negotiations on your behalf and advise you whether to accept the other party's proposed terms rather than let the judge decide. An experienced family law lawyer will be able to tell you the likely result if you choose to litigate the dispute in court rather than accept the other party's offer. In most jurisdictions, this is crucial, because if you choose to litigate rather than accept the other party's offer, you may be ordered to pay the other party's legal costs if the judge's decision is not better than the terms of the offer. The law expects parties to make and accept reasonable settlement offers, and when the judge discovers at the end of the case that an offer was made that should have been accepted (because the offer was the same as or better than the court's decision), the only way for the court to express its displeasure for having wasted time and expense on an unnecessary hearing is to order costs against the party who didn't accept the offer.

How do judges treat litigants who represent themselves?

Do family court judges have any special obligations or responsibilities toward litigants who represent themselves? There is a misconception among many people that if a person doesn't get a lawyer, the judge will "pick up the slack" and protect that person's interests, so no one really needs a lawyer in family court. I cannot tell you how many times words to that effect are said to me by litigants. I have even heard lawyers express resentment that some judges seem to "bend over backward" to assist unrepresented litigants, sometimes at the expense of the other party who is represented by legal counsel. It is important to clarify what the judge's role is.

Family court judges have two major obligations: to ensure that court hearings are fair and to make the best possible decisions for the well-being of the families (especially the children) whose lives we touch. Judges must follow and apply the law. There is no separate set of laws for litigants without lawyers; the same laws and procedural rules apply to all litigants, whether or not they have lawyers. That being said, judges must exercise their discretion to do what is reasonably necessary for fairness to occur, and this can sometimes create the impression that the judge is helping or favouring one side over the other, especially if one party has a lawyer and the other party does not.

Unrepresented and self-represented litigants generally do not know the law or procedure. Consequently, judges spend a great deal of time explaining legal principles and procedures to them. At case conferences, motions and settlement conferences, we often tell them what evidence they are going to need in order to prove or defend a claim. We sometimes make suggestions about settlement offers that should be exchanged. In trials, we sometimes ask questions of witnesses that unrepresented/self-represented parties fail to ask, or rephrase questions that are not asked in the proper form. All of this is done *not* because we are assuming the role of the unrepresented/self-represented party's lawyer or advocate but rather to fulfill the two obligations mentioned above: to be fair and to make good decisions. It can be challenging to provide the necessary assistance to unrepresented/self-represented litigants while at the same time not be perceived as compromising our impartiality. Let me assure you that judges do their very best to strike the appropriate balance at all times.

Sometimes I hear people complain that judges do not do enough to help litigants without lawyers. I believe that judges try their best to make the court case proceed as painlessly and efficiently as possible for *all litigants*. However, there is a limit to what we can do. Judges are impartial, independent decision makers and cannot become advocates for either party. We cannot give legal advice or decide litigation strategy for parties in their court cases. And while I'm at it, we are not counsellors, therapists, spiritual advisers, financial analysts, dating consultants, sex therapists, or magicians either!

Some litigants send letters to the judge in advance of their court hearings, asking for advice or wanting to give the judge some "private" information the other party is not to know about. This is totally improper, as judges cannot communicate with parties individually, and any information a party wishes to give to the judge must first be given to the other party. If the judge were to read such a letter, the case could possibly be transferred to another judge, although usually a copy of the letter would just be given to the other party. As a practical matter, judges rarely receive these kinds of letters because most courts have authorized personnel open the judges' mail. Letters from litigants are returned to them without being seen by the judge.

Have I convinced you?

By now I hope you have been persuaded to hire a lawyer or at least to obtain as much legal advice as possible to help you resolve disputes with your ex-partner. Let's review all of the reasons why you need a lawyer:

1) Family court is not like a television show, nor is it a "walk-in clinic" or a fast-food outlet. You cannot just "tell it to the judge" and get a rapid decision. The fact that no one knows your story better than you do does not qualify you to get that story before the judge in the proper *written* form — or, for that matter, in the proper oral form.

2) A lawyer will determine what information is legally relevant to the issues in dispute.

3) A lawyer will ensure that the hearsay rule is followed and that objections are made on your behalf if the other party tries to present inadmissible evidence. A lawyer will help to ensure that all relevant information is presented to the court as admissible evidence.

4) A lawyer can explain your substantive legal rights and obligations and those of your ex-partner, so that you know what claims each of you are allowed to make.

5) A lawyer can review your situation and help you decide whether your dispute should be resolved using one of the

methods in Chapter 4. You should not start a court case against your ex-partner unless advised to do so by a lawyer.

6) A lawyer knows the proper procedures to follow so that your case is brought to the correct court and proceeds efficiently.

7) A lawyer has the necessary objectivity to assess your circumstances and give you an honest professional opinion on the merits of your claims. If you do go to court, your lawyer will make every effort to keep the litigation free of emotionality and hostility by focusing the negotiations and court hearings in a settlement-oriented direction.

Family law lawyers perform a valuable service to parents dealing with conflicts stemming from separation and divorce. They study for three years in law school, write bar examinations, and receive extensive on-the-job training and continuing education. All of this is done to acquire the necessary knowledge and expertise to help you satisfactorily resolve the most important issues you may ever have to face in your life. Any person who genuinely believes that he/she can navigate the court system as well as or better than a lawyer is seriously misguided, to say the least. If you retain only one message from this book, please let it be this one: get a lawyer!

Can both parties use the same lawyer?

The answer is no. A lawyer cannot represent both parties to a dispute because it is a conflict of interest and would be unethical. It is impossible for the same lawyer to advocate for and protect both parties' rights and interests, because the parties' interests are opposed to each other. For example, if the parties are negotiating over the division of their matrimonial property, each party will want to get as much property or money as possible. If the parties are negotiating a parenting plan, each party will want to have as much time with the child as possible. How could one lawyer make sure that both parties' opposing goals are met?

In addition, all communications between a lawyer and client are confidential and cannot be disclosed by the lawyer to anyone else. If the same lawyer represents both parties, there is a risk that the lawyer might use confidential information received from one party against the interests of the other, and vice versa. In fact, it is improper for a lawyer to represent a party if, at any time in the past, he/she has worked for the other party or for the couple as a family unit. There must be no possibility that a lawyer will make improper use of confidential information received from a client or former client. Consequently, each party needs independent legal advice from his/her own lawyer who has no connection whatsoever to the other party. In addition, the lawyers in the case cannot be affiliated with each other; they must work in separate law firms.

Working it out ourselves: do we still need separate lawyers?

Some couples are able to amicably settle their financial and parenting issues on their own without outside help. They just want a lawyer to "write it up and make it official." While these parents are to be applauded for their maturity and desire to make peace, it is *absolutely essential* that no agreements be signed until each parent has had the opportunity to obtain independent legal advice from *separate* family law lawyers. This applies to marriage contracts, cohabitation agreements, paternity agreements, separation agreements, and any other type of contract entered into between partners or ex-partners. In fact, in my opinion, this admonition applies not only in family law: no one should ever sign any contract without first getting legal advice.

Each ex-partner needs a lawyer to explain his/her legal rights and obligations. Your lawyer will advise you of the practical and legal consequences of the agreement. If the agreement deals with financial matters, you need to know whether you gave and received all required financial disclosure so the agreement reflects both parties' true financial situations. You need to know whether the agreement complies with the law and whether a court would uphold it and enforce it. You need to know whether the agreement is final or open to variation by the court if one or both parties' circumstances change in the future. (For more about this, see Chapter 12.)

The family courts are filled with parties dissatisfied with agreements they entered into at a time when they were emotionally distraught or perhaps feeling pressured. The law expects separating spouses to be fair with each other. If undue influence or duress is exerted by one party against the other, or if a party failed to fully disclose all of his/her assets, or if an agreement is so unfair that it shocks the conscience of the court (lawyers use the term *unconscionable*), your agreement could be set aside or varied by the court. This could even happen many years after the agreement was entered into. You can imagine how disruptive and traumatic such a result can be for ex-partners who may have assumed the agreement would remain in effect for the rest of their lives. They may have remarried or reorganized their finances in reliance on the agreement, only to find that the agreement is no longer binding. (This is discussed further in Chapter 12.)

It should also be pointed out that the court is never bound by parental agreements relating to custody, access, and child support. This is because these are rights of the child and the court has the overriding authority to ensure that all arrangements affecting children are in their best interests. Parents cannot bargain away their children's rights. Assume, for example, that Parent A and Parent B have agreed that Parent A will have sole custody of the child and Parent B will pay no child support in return for never seeing the child again. If in the future Parent A decides to seek child support from Parent B, or if Parent B decides he/she would like to have visitation with the child, the court will consider their applications and will not hold the parents to their agreement. This is another reason why it is important to get legal advice before entering into any agreements; you need a lawyer to tell you whether your agreement would meet the "best interests" test if it were ever to be reviewed by a court, and whether the terms are enforceable. (For a complete discussion of the factors considered in a legal determination of the best interests of the child, see Chapter 6.)

Paralegals

I mentioned above that legal fees can be expensive. Is it a good idea to hire a paralegal rather than a lawyer? A paralegal is not a lawyer but may have some post-secondary school training in legal procedures. Some paralegals work in law firms and provide clerical and administrative assistance to lawyers. Other paralegals are self-employed. Some jurisdictions have laws stating the training that paralegals must receive and the kinds of work they can do. In some of these jurisdictions, paralegals must be licensed and are regulated by professional organizations similar to those that oversee the legal profession.

Even if the law in your jurisdiction allows paralegals to perform family law services, you should proceed with caution before hiring a paralegal. Paralegals do not receive the same training as lawyers and may not recognize all of the legal issues arising from your situation. As paralegals are not lawyers, they cannot give legal advice. Also, the confidentiality rules applying to lawyer-client communications (called *solicitor-client privilege*) do not normally apply to client-paralegal communications unless the law in your jurisdiction provides this protection. Unlike lawyers, paralegals in most jurisdictions do not have an automatic right to represent litigants in court. They must first obtain the court's permission to do so. The judge will ask the paralegal questions about his/her training, experience, degree of supervision by a lawyer, and whether he/she has malpractice insurance.

I have met some excellent paralegals who have received intensive training in family law and court procedures and who work under the close supervision of family law lawyers. I have met other paralegals who had no legal or procedural knowledge and who had no business whatsoever offering assistance to family court litigants. If you are considering hiring a paralegal, inquire whether your jurisdiction has regulations in effect governing paralegals, particularly in the area of family law. Go to your local family court and ask if paralegals are allowed to represent litigants. Find out whether the law in your jurisdiction protects the confidentiality of client communications. Inquire about the paralegal's training and experience *in family law,* and ask whether the paralegal works under the supervision of a family law lawyer. Ask the paralegal whether he/she has malpractice insurance and, if so, the amount of the coverage. Ask the paralegal when he/she will next be in court so that you can go to court and watch the hearing. You will be able to tell a lot about the paralegal's competence by observing how he/she conducts him/herself in court (assuming he/she is granted permission to represent the litigant).

Choosing a lawyer: get a family law specialist

The law is a complex and varied discipline. Although law students take a variety of courses in law school and write bar examinations in a number of subjects before being licensed to practice law, it is rare for a lawyer to practice in many fields. This is because it is difficult to remain apprised of the constant changes in legislation, procedural rules, and case law in each subject area. Consequently, most lawyers choose to specialize in the subject areas that interest them the most. Some common areas of specialization are labour law, corporate law, real estate law, wills and estates, civil litigation, entertainment law, environmental law, patents and trademarks, medical malpractice, insurance law, bankruptcy law, criminal law, and, yes, family law.

I strongly believe that parents involved in family law disputes should, if at all possible, hire lawyers who specialize in family law. I say this for the same reason that family doctors refer patients to specialists in the medical field: professionals who specialize in one field become experts in that subject, and it is always best to have an expert working for you. Family law specialists not only have intensive and current knowledge of family law but are totally familiar with the inner workings of the court system. They have the expertise to assess the merits of your claim and your ex-partner's claim. They probably know each other because they have likely worked with each other on many cases (assuming both parents hire lawyers from the same city or town). A good working relationship between lawyers who respect and trust each other is incredibly helpful in resolving disputes smoothly. Family law specialists also know their local judiciary and usually can reliably predict the likely outcome of your court case, because they have litigated similar issues in front of the same judges many times. They also have the experience and judgment to advise you on whether you and your ex-partner should be availing yourselves of one of the alternative dispute resolution mechanisms referred to in Chapter 4. If one of those mechanisms is going to be used, they know who the best mediators and arbitrators are in your community. They also know how to connect you and your children with the appropriate community resources such as counsellors, parenting coaches, access supervisors, custody assessors, and property valuators.

It is not always possible to retain a lawyer who specializes in family law. Some small cities and towns do not have family law specialists — or there may be only one in your town and your ex-partner may already have hired him/her. Some specialists charge fees you may consider unaffordable. If you are unable to hire a family law specialist, make sure you hire a lawyer who has significant family law experience. Don't be afraid to ask the lawyer what his/her experience is in the family law field. Ask him/her what percentage of his/her law practice consists of family law work. Although there are no hard and fast rules, I would suggest that a lawyer whose practice is comprised of at least 50 per cent family law clients probably has a good working knowledge and sufficient experience to represent you adequately, depending on the complexity of your case.

Finding a lawyer

Finding a family law specialist is generally not difficult, as most bar associations and regulatory bodies governing the legal profession maintain lists of lawyers who have been certified or who have self-identified as specialists. Call them and ask for a list of family law specialists. Some jurisdictions also have local family lawyers' associations, and they may provide members of the public with lists of members. Such lists are an excellent place to start. Many lawyers have their own Web sites that give a great deal of information regarding their approach to family dispute resolution and client service.

The best way to find a good family law lawyer is through word of mouth. Ask people you know who have separated from their partners if they were satisfied with their lawyers, and, if so, get the lawyers' contact information. Ask each person what services the lawyers provided (mediation, arbitration, litigation, negotiating a separation agreement, and so on), how long it took to resolve the issues, and the amount charged (hourly rate and total fees paid). Ask if the lawyer was easily accessible by telephone and/or e-mail and whether the client was kept informed at all times of the progress of his/her case.

If you do not know anyone who has personally used the services of a family law lawyer, contact any community or social service agency that provides assistance to parents and children who have experienced family breakdown. Sometimes these organizations have lists of family law lawyers.

You might also consult any lawyer you may know. For example, if you have hired a lawyer in the past to conduct a real estate transaction, write your will, or handle some other legal matter, ask him/her to recommend a family law lawyer. Many lawyers who do not practise in a particular field know colleagues in other fields and can steer clients in the right direction.

If none of these suggestions is possible, then go to your local family court. You are likely to see numerous lawyers waiting for their cases to be heard. Approach some of the lawyers and ask for their business cards. Tell them you are looking to hire a family law lawyer and you wish to make an appointment. Do not expect a lengthy conversation with the lawyer in the waiting area at the courthouse, as he/she is there to conduct business for another client and will not likely have time to conduct a full consultation with you. If you are permitted to enter the courtroom, watch the proceedings and make note of the lawyers whose conduct impress you. You will learn a great deal about a lawyer's personality, advocacy style, and reputation from watching how he/she conducts him/herself in court. Does he/she seem well prepared? Does he/she treat the other party's lawyer and the judge with courtesy and respect, or is he/she overly aggressive, argumentative, or obnoxious? Is the lawyer presenting practical, settlement-oriented solutions to the court? Do the lawyer's submissions make sense to you? Do you get the impression that he/she is respected by his/her colleagues and the judge, or did the judge have to correct the lawyer on points of law, ethics, and procedure? These are the factors you should be looking for.

Hiring a lawyer

Don't be afraid to "shop around" for a lawyer. Make appointments with several lawyers and hire the one who you feel will best meet your needs. When you make the appointment, ask what documents you will need to bring with you, what the fee will be for the initial consultation, and when payment will be expected. It is a good idea to write out your questions ahead of time.

When you meet with a lawyer, four important things should happen:

1) Give the lawyer all the information he/she has asked for, including all details you think are important. Answer all his/her questions fully and honestly.
2) Tell the lawyer what you would like to achieve so the lawyer can tell you if your goals are realistic. For example, which parent do you want the child to live with? If you are not asking for the child to live with you, what visitation schedule do you want? Will you want child or spousal support? Are there specific items of property that you want to keep? Do you want a restraining order to keep the other parent away from you because you fear for your safety? If you and

your ex-partner have incurred joint debts, how do you propose they be paid?

3) Listen carefully to the lawyer's advice. He/she will tell you
three crucial things:

(a) your rights and obligations (in other words, whether you
have a good case to get what you asked for in #2);

(b) your ex-partner's rights and obligations; and

(c) the specific action plan he/she proposes in order to obtain
the results you seek (court action or one of the alternatives
discussed in Chapter 4).

4) The lawyer will explain the billing procedure. Most lawyers
charge in the range of $200 to $500 per hour, plus expenses
for such things as photocopies and court filing fees (called
disbursements), plus tax. A client will usually be required to
make a substantial deposit of several thousand dollars (called
a *retainer*) before a lawyer will agree to take a case. Some
law firms have junior lawyers, law students, and paralegals
on staff who perform certain non-crucial tasks at less expensive hourly rates than the higher-priced lawyer who has been
retained, in order to minimize the client's legal costs. Be
aware that it is impossible for a lawyer to predict with certainty what your total legal fees will be; the total will depend
on how much work the lawyer will have to do on your behalf
to resolve the disputed issues. This, in turn, will depend on
the positions you and your ex-partner are taking regarding
each issue. Obviously, the more issues that you and your ex-
partner cannot agree on, and the longer the dispute lasts, the
more work your lawyer (and your ex-partner's lawyer) will
have to do, and the higher the fees will be.

You may not be able to achieve all of the above steps at your first
meeting. The lawyer may require further information or documentation. The lawyer may need to have a discussion with your ex-partner's
lawyer to identify the issues in dispute. The lawyer may need to conduct some legal research before giving you a legal opinion on the
merits of your claim or your ex-partner's claim.

Once the lawyer has given you the information in #3, how do you
decide whether to accept the legal advice and hire the lawyer?

Sometimes when hiring a professional, one asks for references from other clients. Unfortunately this is not generally possible in the legal profession because lawyers are bound by strict confidentiality rules that do not permit them to disclose clients' identities without their consents. If you have not been referred to the lawyer by someone whose opinion you trust, it can be difficult to know whether to accept the legal advice you are being given, especially if that advice is not what you were hoping to receive (for example, if the lawyer is telling you that you are not entitled to ownership of your ex-partner's fabulous château on the French Riviera!).

In choosing a lawyer, keep in mind that your goal should be to get the best possible legal advice, not to find someone who agrees with you. The only way to know if you have been given good legal advice is to get a second opinion from another lawyer. This second lawyer should be a family law specialist and therefore an expert. This can be expensive, but if you have serious doubts about the quality of the legal advice you have received, I cannot think of a better way to test that advice.

If your lawyer is advising you to start a court action, ask the lawyer when he/she will next be appearing in court and tell him/her that you want to observe the hearing (if this is allowed where you live). I mentioned earlier the factors you should be looking for. If, after seeing your lawyer's "advocacy style," you would feel comfortable having him/her as your advocate and spokesperson, then you have probably found a lawyer you will be happy with.

How do I assess my lawyer's performance?

Judges only deal with lawyers who conduct litigation. Lawyers who practice collaborative law or who work exclusively in mediation or arbitration do not come to court, and therefore I cannot comment on the factors used to assess their performance. I can, however, comment on the qualities and indicators that constitute good performance by family law lawyers who litigate in court.

As with all professionals, there is a wide variety of competence among lawyers. I have seen excellent lawyers, I have seen incompetent lawyers, and I have seen everything in between. I am pleased to report that the vast majority of lawyers whom I have encountered in my career have been highly competent and dedicated to their clients. They are a credit to the legal profession and to the communities in which they serve.

In my opinion, a good litigation lawyer should

1) Know the law. There is no excuse for a lawyer who has not kept up with changes in the statutes, court rules, and case law. It is unacceptable to miss limitation periods (court filing deadlines) or to file incomplete documentation.

2) Be well prepared. Court appearances are time-consuming and expensive for clients, so something meaningful should be achieved at each court date. A lawyer should know what he/she wants to accomplish at each court appearance and communicate this to the other party at least several weeks before the court date. Both parties' lawyers should have intensive discussions and negotiations well in advance of the court date to narrow the issues and decide how best to use the court time allocated to them. There should be no surprises sprung on the other party in the courtroom (for example, requests for court orders being made for the first time without prior notice to the other party, or new evidence being given to the court without first having been given to the other party well in advance so that they could prepare a response).

3) Be professional and courteous to other lawyers at all times, and retain his/her objectivity. He/she must not become emotionally embroiled in the dispute, and never turn the litigation into a dispute between the lawyers. I have had cases in which the lawyers spent the entire time arguing and hurling complaints and insults at each other instead of addressing their clients' issues. This is not helpful to the clients or the court, and it reflects badly on the legal profession.

4) Be practical, child-focused (in custody and access cases), and settlement-oriented. Look for solutions, not problems. Encourage clients to focus on the future rather than rehash the past. Lawyers can be major role models in teaching clients to adopt mature attitudes and behaviour.

5) Resort to court action only when it is truly necessary. (This

is discussed more completely in Chapters 2, 3, and 4.)

6) Communicate with his/her client. Give clear legal advice, with concrete options. Get firm instructions from the client and follow them. Make sure the client understands the goals and likely outcomes of each court appearance, including the possibility of a costs order being made for or against the client. Resolve misunderstandings and communication problems with the client away from the courtroom and in private, not in front of the judge.

You have the right to expect that your lawyer will conduct him/herself in accordance with these points. If you feel your lawyer is not doing so, discuss this with him/her. If the problem is not rectified to your satisfaction, you may have to consider changing lawyers. This can be very expensive and disruptive to the progress of your case, but if you are truly unhappy with your lawyer's performance, you may have no other option. You should also know that if your lawyer feels that there has been a breakdown in the lawyer-client relationship, impairing his/her ability to properly represent you, he/she may terminate the relationship. If a court case is already in progress, a court order may be required to do this. Judges usually will allow a lawyer to leave the case (this is called *being removed from the record* or *being relieved from the case*), because it is generally not appropriate to compel a lawyer to continue to represent a client who has lost confidence in him/her.

I have told you what constitutes a good lawyer. It is equally important to know what constitutes a *good client*. Your lawyer can only help you if you take his/her advice — even if you would rather not. As stated above, if you have doubts about the accuracy of the legal advice you have received, get a second opinion from another lawyer who is a family law specialist. However, once your lawyer's advice has been confirmed, *follow that advice*. The reason you hire a lawyer in the first place is because he/she has the knowledge and experience to advise you of your rights and obligations. Too many times, clients fire their lawyers and end up representing themselves because their lawyers didn't tell them what they wanted to hear. I have had countless cases in which parties hired and fired numerous lawyers because they were not prepared to accept the legal advice that was being given to them — advice that was appropriate and that should have been followed. The lawyer's job is to tell you the truth, even if it hurts. In the long run, it is better to take your lawyer's advice and do the right thing than to be ordered by a judge to do it, and then be ordered to pay the other party's legal costs stemming from your unreasonableness. Remember: maturity is the name of the game, and being mature means following legal advice.

---

1   In jurisdictions in which all litigants are entitled to government-funded legal counsel, the problem of unrepresented litigants does not exist.

2   Anne-Marie Langan, "Threatening the Balance of the Scales of Justice: Unrepresented Litigants in the Family Courts of Ontario," (2005) 30 Queen's L.J. 825.

3   Philip Slayton, "The Self-representation Problem," *Canadian Lawyer Magazine*, Nov./Dec. 2007, p. 30.

CHAPTER SIX

CUSTODY AND ACCESS DISPUTES: "THE BEST INTERESTS OF THE CHILD"

ASIDE FROM CHILD PROTECTION CASES WHERE PARENTAL RIGHTS ARE BEING TERMINATED DUE TO CHILD ABUSE AND NEGLECT, THE MOST HEART-WRENCHING AND TRAGIC CASES WE SEE IN FAMILY COURT ARE HIGH-CONFLICT CUSTODY AND ACCESS DISPUTES. All too often, parents are so filled with hatred and vindictiveness that they keep the litigation going as a means of torturing each other without the slightest concern for the effect of their immature behaviour on their children. As I've mentioned, some custody and access disputes last throughout a child's entire childhood — the parents don't stop litigating until the child grows up! They turn every long weekend, vacation period, and special occasion into "all or nothing" battles. They seek retribution for lateness and cancellations. They ask the court to impose a multitude of conditions and restrictions limiting what each other can do with the child and dictating which relatives and friends can be introduced to the child. I have had parents litigate over what television shows their children should be allowed to watch and what toys they should be allowed to play with. I even had a case in which *neither* parent wanted the children on the weekends, as each one wanted free time for dating. Imagine having to decide which of two unwilling parents should have to spend time with their children! For parents who are intent on keeping a dispute alive, no issue is too small to litigate.

These parents are oblivious to the impact on their children of being caught in the middle of a relentless tug of war. Any psychologist, social worker, or teacher who works with these unfortunate children can tell you the emotional damage they endure is significant and potentially long-lasting. In my opinion, the fact that parents are separated is not in itself damaging to children. Nor is the fact that parents have conflicts with each other. The damage to children comes from their *exposure* to the conflict. Parents must have the maturity to insulate their children from the conflict by not talking to them about it and by not arguing or fighting in front of them. Tragically, in most long-lasting, high conflict custody and access cases that I have seen, the parents have not acted maturely, and their children have paid a huge emotional price.

As I mentioned in Chapter 5, the most surprising aspect of custody and access litigation is the relatively minor focus placed by many parents on the children. Parents should be giving the court as much information as possible about the children's relationships, routines, aptitudes, and needs. Instead, a great many parents choose to attack various aspects of each other's lives, such as their characters, fidelity, financial and business transactions, relatives, new partners, choice of friends, and even their hobbies. Much of the evidence presented has nothing to do with the children. Parents who take this approach create the impression that their custody litigation is a struggle for power, control, and vengeance rather than a sincere effort to arrive at the best possible parenting plan for their children. Mistakenly, these parents are not giving the court evidence *relevant* to the custody and access issues: whom the child will live with, what the visitation schedule will be with the other parent, and how major decisions regarding the child will be made.

In custody and access cases, judges need the most complete and reliable information about the children's needs and the parents' abilities to meet those needs, in order to make the best possible decisions for children. In this chapter, I will discuss the factors considered by family courts in making custody and access decisions. This should assist you in the all-important task of ensuring that the evidence you present will be *relevant*.

Best interests of the children

In most jurisdictions, there is one fundamental legal principle governing custody and access cases: the judge must decide what is in the best interests of the child. In some jurisdictions, the definition of *best interests of the child* is found in legislation, and in others, the meaning of the term has evolved through judicial decisions (called *case law*). Either way, this term encompasses many aspects that permit the court to craft individual decisions that meet each child's needs and circumstances. Here, in no particular order, are the most commonly referred-to components of a best interests of the child analysis. There is no rule making one factor more important than any other. The weight applied to these factors in any given case depends on each family's specific circumstances.

Child's emotional bonds

A custody and access order dictates which parent a child will live with and how often the child will be with the other parent. In making these decisions, the court must take into account the love, affection, and emotional ties between the child and each parent and family member involved in the child's care and upbringing. A child's strongest emotional bond is usually with his/her primary caregiver — the person who has played the major role in the child's daily care. For example, if one parent has been a stay-at-home caregiver to the child while the other parent has been at work five days a week, the child will likely be most bonded to the stay-at-home parent. This does not necessarily mean that the stay-at-home parent will be granted custody, but it is an important factor to be considered.

Clearly the fact that one parent is out of the home five days a week is not an indication that that parent loves or cares about the child any less than the stay-at-home parent. Nor does it necessarily mean that the stay-at-home parent has the best parenting skills. However, it is generally desirable to minimize the effects of parental separation on children as much as possible and to maintain consistency in their daily care and routines. Chances are that by the time a separated couple gets in front of a judge, their child will have been through quite enough disruption. Courts are understandably reluctant to change a child's primary caregiver unless there is a good reason to do so.

In many families, both parents work full-time and their children are in daycare or school on weekdays. In the evenings and on weekends, the parents may have been equally involved in caring for the children, in which case the children may be equally bonded to both parents. Given the fact that parenting skills are assessed on a gender-neutral basis — that is, the law treats mothers and fathers equally — neither parent is more entitled than the other to have custody solely by reason of his/her gender. Consequently, when a child is equally bonded to both parents, the custody decision must be based on other factors, including the ones discussed in this chapter. In appropriate circumstances, it may be possible to arrive at a shared parenting or joint custody arrangement (see Chapter 7).

I have had cases in which the children were in the care of a live-in nanny much more than they were with their very busy parents who worked long hours. In some of those cases, I had the distinct impression that the children were more emotionally bonded to their nannies than to their parents. Although the nannies were not claiming custody, I had to consider the nanny's role in each parent's parenting plan.

Any discussion of a child's emotional bonds must include the child's relationship to other family members besides parents. Children's bonds with their siblings, grandparents, aunts, uncles, and cousins are all important. The proximity and potential involvement of the child's relatives on both sides of the family are relevant factors to be considered in assessing a parenting plan. I have even had cases in which a child's emotional bond to a beloved pet played an important role in the custody dispute. In one case involving a twelve-year-old child who dearly loved her dog, Parent A had moved in with a relative who was allergic to dogs. Parent B remained in the family home and was willing to keep the dog. A child psychologist was providing therapy to this emotionally fragile child to help her cope with the family breakdown. The psychologist testified that the unconditional love and companionship provided by the dog was beneficial and therapeutic to the child during this difficult stage in her life. I actually had the impression that the child was more emotionally bonded to her dog than to either parent! You can guess the result in that case.

I have mentioned that a child's emotional bond with his/her siblings is important. In most cases a sibling bond will last longer than a parent-child bond because in the natural order of events, parents will die before their children. It is generally considered desirable to maintain and nurture a child's sibling relationships by having siblings raised together in the same household. However, some parents propose that custody of several children be divided: for example, Parent A gets custody of one child and Parent B gets custody of the other child. This is called *split custody*. It is sad that some children have to cope not only with their parents' separation but also with being separated from their siblings. A split custody proposal should be made only on the advice of a family law lawyer. Most courts will be reluctant to agree to such an arrangement without persuasive evidence that *all* of the children will benefit more by living apart than by living together, and that they will have sufficient opportunities to spend quality time together.

Sometimes a custody dispute is not between the child's parents but rather between a parent and other relatives. I have had cases involving disputes between a parent and a grandparent or between a parent and a step-parent. In some jurisdictions, biological parents have greater rights than step-parents and relatives. In other jurisdictions, such as the one where I preside, no person has an automatic upper hand in a custody dispute. Although the child's biological connection to a custody claimant is an important factor to be considered, it does not create a presumption of entitlement to custody: in such jurisdictions, the court must consider *all* of the circumstances and grant custody to the person who can best meet the child's needs. For more information about how custody law in your area treats biological parents in relation to step-parents and relatives, consult a lawyer.

I have had cases in which both parents were deceased, and relatives from both sides of the family were seeking custody of the children. Imagine how devastating it must be for a child to lose both parents and then be caught in a tug of war between extended family members. In such cases, the emotional bond factor is very important because of the desirability of placing these very traumatized children with people to whom they are most attached.

In one tragic case, Parent A murdered Parent B and was sentenced to life imprisonment. The four-year-old child of this relationship was the subject of a custody dispute between Parent A's mother and Parent B's mother. You can imagine the hostility that Parent B's family felt toward Parent A and Parent A's family, even though Parent A's family was not responsible for Parent A's conduct and in no way condoned it. To complicate matters, Parent A's family felt that the child should regularly be taken to the jail to visit Parent A, and Parent B's family felt that the child should never see Parent A again. I told the parties that the court system, which was created to deal with *legal* problems, was not the best place for them because their problems were not really of a legal nature. What they needed was intensive counselling and therapeutic support to help them move beyond their grief and anger. This would enable them to focus on the child's need to develop and strengthen emotional bonds with *all* members of a *united* family. The parties were referred to mediation, and a mutually agreeable joint parenting plan was arrived at. The plan incorporated family counselling, and the child was engaged in therapy with a child psychologist, who would also assist with the very delicate issue of determining what relationship, if any, the child should have with Parent A.

Status quo

Another important aspect in determining a child's best interests is the length of time the child has lived in a stable home environment. This is often referred to as the status quo factor, or, simply stated, what the situation has been up until now, both before and since the separation. If the court is asked to decide custody several months (or sometimes years) after the parents separated, it is particularly important to consider the living arrangements that have been in place since the date of separation. For example, at the time of separation one parent may have moved out of the home with the child, in which case the child had to adjust to a new home and possibly a new school. Or the child may have remained in the family home with one parent. Sometimes both parents move out of the home and establish new residences. In making custody decisions, courts try to minimize the disruption to the child's life caused by the separation. So, if before the court is asked to make its decision, the child has already had to move once and is now settled into his/her new home, there is something to be said for not making the child move again.

This is why temporary custody and access orders obtained in motions (explained in Chapter 2) are so important: they establish a status quo that may be difficult to change. Obviously, the longer a temporary situation exists, the more difficult it may be to persuade the court to change it. There must usually be a good reason to disrupt a child's living arrangements, especially if the court is of the view that the temporary arrangement has worked out well for the child. For example, assume that at a motion early in the court case, Parent A is granted temporary custody and Parent B gets access to the child on alternate weekends and one evening during the week. The parties are unable to reach a final agreement, as Parent B wants custody. Due to court backlogs, a trial is held one year after Parent A got temporary custody. In most cases, the fact that the child has been living with Parent A for such a long time will work in favour of Parent A's custody proposal. In order for Parent B's custody proposal to succeed, Parent B will likely have to convince the judge on a balance of probabilities (see Chapter 2) that the benefit to the child of moving to his/her home will outweigh the disruption caused to the child by the change in residence. It is primarily for this reason that trials so rarely occur in family court: the temporary orders resulting from motions very often determine the final outcome of the case.

Parenting plans

Each parent's plan for the child's care and upbringing must be considered. The court will compare the parents' housing, schooling, and daycare arrangements, as well as the extracurricular activities in which each parent plans to engage the child. In assessing the parents' plans, the court will be trying to determine which parent is best equipped to meet the child's needs.

As mentioned in Chapter 2, the court is not bound by either parent's plan and may impose a different arrangement that it considers to be best for the child. For example, assume that Parent A, who lives alone and works weekdays from nine to five, plans to place the two-year-old child in daycare and proposes that Parent B has the child on alternate weekends. Parent B lives with his/her retired parents and works on a three-week rotating shift schedule of days, afternoons, and nights. Parent B's plan is to have his/her parents take care of the child while he/she is at work. The court may decide that it is in the child's best interests to live with Parent A, but instead of going to daycare, the child should be with Parent B's parents when Parent A is at work. So, in a way, there is the potential for three parenting plans in every custody case: Parent A's, Parent B's, and a possible plan devised by the judge!

Stability

Everyone agrees that children need consistency and stability in their lives. In examining parenting plans, the court will consider the permanence and stability of the family unit in which it is proposed the child will live. Upon separation, many parents move in temporarily with relatives or friends. Some parents find new partners and move in with them and their children, creating blended family units. The court will be looking for the most stable living arrangement for the child, to minimize the risk of further moves and disruption.

If you have entered into a new relationship, you must consider the impact of this relationship on your child, particularly if you are living with your new partner. Children need time to adjust to parental separation, particularly if they are old enough to understand the situation. They need to settle into a new routine that will allow them to spend quality time with both parents. I am constantly surprised by the rapidity with which some parents embark on new relationships, before they have given themselves and their children enough time to heal from the emotional trauma of the separation. Before you move in with a new partner and impose this new relationship on your child, you need to be sure that this living arrangement will be happy, stable, and long-term if you are going to ask the court to grant you custody. Let's face it: parents who come to family court already have a track record of at least one unsuccessful relationship; how can anyone be sure that the next relationship will last? We must proceed cautiously when a child's stability and permanency planning are at stake. Be aware that any parenting plan that involves a new partner has to be carefully considered.

Some parents find new partners who live in other jurisdictions, and they want to move with the child to some faraway place to live with their new partners. Some parents want to move away to be near their families, or because they have found a good job there. These cases (called *mobility* or *relocation* cases) are among the most complex and emotionally intense of all custody cases, because it is very difficult to arrive at compromises when one parent wants to take the child a great distance away from the other parent. The court must examine all of the circumstances, with the primary focus being the impact on the child of the proposed move. If you are involved in a mobility case, you will almost certainly need a lawyer to help you compile and present the evidence required to make or respond to a request to move your child's residence to another jurisdiction. Remember that mobility cases, like all cases involving the best interests of children, are decided on the basis of what is best for the child, not what is best for the parents.

Parenting skills

A major factor in the determination of a child's best interests is the parenting skills of each parent claiming custody. There is a wide range of skills that children need their parents to possess and exercise, everything from basic caregiving skills (feeding, bathing, diaper changing, making sure children get enough sleep), to organizational skills (getting children to and from school, making sure homework is completed, meeting the children's healthcare needs), to socialization skills (ensuring that children receive appropriate intellectual, social, and cultural stimulation and community involvement through extracurricular activities). The court will be comparing the parents' abilities to give the child the safest, healthiest, and happiest childhood possible.

If you have read the preceding chapters, it should not surprise you to learn once again that the all-important concept of *maturity* plays a prominent role in any discussion of parenting ability. A parent with good parenting skills puts his/her child's needs ahead of his/her own by demonstrating the ability and willingness to make peace with the other parent for the sake of the child. A parent with good parenting skills will understand the child's need to have a loving relationship with *both* parents and will give the child emotional permission to love the other parent by not speaking negatively about the other parent to the child. In other words, if you are seeking custody, your parenting plan should contemplate significant involvement by the other parent in the child's life and show how you plan to foster a good relationship between the child and the other parent.

As mentioned in Chapter 3, there are some parents who should have restricted contact (or in severe cases, no contact) with their children because the parents' behaviour creates risks to the children's well-being. As a general rule, a parent's behaviour is relevant in a custody and access dispute only if it relates to his/her ability to act as a parent. For example, the fact that a parent may have been sexually unfaithful probably tells us nothing about his/her relationship with his/her child. However, a parent who exercises poor judgment (for example, sending a seven-year-old child alone on a city bus to school so the child can "get more independent") would definitely be problematic. You should not try to minimize or eliminate the other parent's role in the child's life unless advised to do so by a family law lawyer or social worker employed by a child protection agency.

One final word about parenting skills. Although we are living in the twenty-first century, there are some people who believe that mothers have inherently better parenting skills than fathers, especially with young infants. Some people believe that girls need to be raised by their mothers and boys should be raised by their fathers. Some people believe that homosexuals, bisexuals, and trans-gendered people cannot be good parents, or that households run by same-sex couples are somehow inferior to those run by opposite-sex couples. These beliefs are mostly based on generalizations, prejudicial myths, or stereotypes that have no place in family law. All people are entitled to equality under the law. Each parent is a unique individual, with the right to have his/her parenting abilities assessed on the basis of his/her unique personality and skills. Similarly, each child is a unique individual with his/her own specific character, gifts, and needs.

Some people believe that a child must be raised by parents who are of the same race, culture, or religion as the child. I believe that each family's circumstances are different and special, requiring individually crafted solutions that work for them. It is certainly true that factors such as race, culture, and religion are relevant and important to provide a full picture of a family's dynamic and to provide much-needed information about a child's heritage, which should be nurtured and preserved. However, while these factors are to be respected, they should never be the most important issues in a custody decision. Love, especially between parents and their children, is a universal attribute that should transcend every label or category that people may assign to themselves or each other — and, ultimately, love should be at the core of every family court decision regarding children.

Children's views and preferences
If a child is of sufficient age and maturity to express his/her views and preferences, most jurisdictions allow the court to consider them in

assessing the child's best interests. How is this done? Some parents agree to jointly hire a child psychologist or qualified social worker to conduct an assessment. In some jurisdictions, there is a government agency that employs social workers who have special training and expertise in ascertaining children's wishes in the very delicate question of which parent's custody plan is preferable to the child. Some courts are permitted or required to appoint government-funded lawyers (sometimes called *law guardians* or *guardians ad litem*) to represent children and advocate their wishes in custody and access cases. In some jurisdictions, the judge is permitted to interview the child privately.

As you might expect, the task of ascertaining a child's wishes is fraught with difficulties. For one thing, how do we know if a child has reached a sufficient level of maturity to understand the dynamics of the family breakdown and to evaluate both parents' custody plans in terms of his/her own best interests? Most adolescents and teenagers are capable of expressing their views and preferences, but what about children under twelve years old? Each child's cognitive development and maturity level must be individually assessed, and only a child psychologist, qualified social worker, or other professional with special expertise in dealing with children can reliably make such an assessment. The court must be satisfied that a young child is sufficiently mature to understand and evaluate the competing parenting plans and the consequences of choosing one over the other. Without this assurance, the court may not be inclined to apply much weight to a young child's views and preferences.

Another challenge is the thorny question of whether the views and preferences being expressed by the child are truly his/her own independent thoughts. Following a parental separation, many parents involve the children in their disputes and place incredible pressure on them to "take sides." They denigrate and bad-mouth each other in front of their children, encouraging them to dislike and disrespect the other parent. They bribe, manipulate, and emotionally blackmail their children into expressing a preference for one parent over the other. This is one of the most immature and cruel things a parent can do because it places children in a no-win "conflict of loyalties" situation. Children are innocent victims in a family breakdown and should be protected from parental conflicts. They want to love and be loved by both parents; they should not have to choose between them. In my opinion, it is a form of child abuse when a parent tries to poison and brainwash a child against the other parent. Unfortunately, family court judges see this all too often.

It is a very frequent occurrence in my courtroom that each parent will tell me emphatically and with great confidence that the children want to live with him/her. Both parents are probably telling me the truth, in the sense that they are repeating what the children have told each of them separately. Children want to be loved and do not want to disappoint either parent, so they will tell each one what he/she wants to hear — what else would you expect from a child who is caught up in a toxic tug of war? When I am confronted with this situation, I always ask each parent to tell me which child he/she loves the most (if they have more than one child). I have never yet met a parent able to answer that question, even when I persist and urge them to give me an answer. Then I tell them, "You are adults, yet you are not able to tell me which of your children you love the most. But you expect your children, who are not yet fully mature, to decide which parent they love the most. Do you think you are being fair to your children by making them choose between you?" I wonder if these parents get the point I am trying to make.

Determining whether a child's stated views and preferences are truly his/her own is accomplished with assistance from professionals who have the necessary expertise in dealing with children. Sometimes the parents have behaved so outrageously that it is obvious the child is simply echoing what he/she has been told to say. I have had cases in which parents wanted to give me letters written by the child — in the parent's handwriting! I have had cases where young children who could not yet read and write were able to recount every detail of the parents' financial disputes. I have had cases in which young children used words such as abusive, egomaniacal, and harassment but could not explain what these words meant. I have even had cases in which a child began an interview with a social worker (before even sitting down and being asked one question) by enthusiastically spouting a well-rehearsed speech spewing venomous insults about one parent — and then proudly telling the social worker that he/she had spent many hours memorizing what the other parent had taught him/her to say! Remember, children are children!

Obviously, the court will not place any weight on a child's views and preferences if it finds these wishes do not reflect the child's true feelings. More importantly, if the court finds that you have coached or pressured a child in the expression of his/her views — or for that matter, if you have in any other way tried to alienate the child from the other parent — this will be a factor against you in deciding which plan is in the child's best interests.

There are a few other things that parents should not do unless instructed by a lawyer or the judge:

1) Do not get your children to write letters to the judge. Chances are, the judge will not read them because there is no way to know the circumstances under which such letters were written. Besides, the fact that you believe it is acceptable for your children to be aware of the parental dispute, let alone play a role in it by writing a letter, will speak volumes about your poor judgment and immaturity. For that matter, your children should not be writing letters to anyone else involved in the case, such as lawyers, mediators, or assessors.

2) Do not bring your children to court. Children should be shielded from the parental conflict, not playing a role in it. They should be in school, not in a courtroom witnessing their parents arguing with each other in front of a judge.

In most jurisdictions, the judge has the discretion to interview a child privately. When I was new in my job, I tried this a few times and found that every child gave me the same message: "I want my parents to get back together so I can live with both of them." It is heartbreaking to try to explain to a child that this is one wish that cannot be granted, not even by a court.

With great respect to those who feel differently, I believe that as a general rule, judges should not interview children in custody and access cases. Judges may not have the necessary training and expertise to put a child at ease in a courthouse setting, in order to hear the child's genuine views and preferences. In addition, one interview may not be enough to get the full picture; it is just a snapshot of how the child is feeling at that moment. It would probably be necessary to interview the child several times to get to know the child, understand the context of what he/she is saying, and see whether his/her expressed wishes are consistently held. I also believe that a judicial interview can place too much pressure on a child, who might mistakenly believe that he/she is responsible for making the final decision. Imagine the interrogation and retribution the child may face at the hands of his/her parents after the interview is over and the judge delivers a decision.

One final word about children's wishes. Please keep in mind that decisions regarding the best interests of children should be made by adults (ideally their parents), not by the children themselves. If the parents cannot agree on a parenting plan, a judge will decide the issue. If the court has been advised of the child's views and preferences, this evidence will be considered along with all of the other evidence in the case. The judge will decide how much importance to place on the child's wishes in relation to the rest of the factors that must be considered. As a general rule, the older the child, the greater the weight that will be applied to his/her wishes. Obviously, the court will not want to force a teenager to live where he/she does not want to live, because it can be difficult if not impossible to enforce such an order. However, in the case of younger children, no one should have the mistaken impression that the child's wishes — even assuming they are genuine — will necessarily determine the outcome. I regularly hear parents claim that their young toddlers should not be forced to visit the other parent if they do not want to go. Would these parents allow a three-year-old child to make any other important decisions for him/herself? What if a six-year-old child decided not to go to school, or to eat only candy, or to decide his/her own bedtime? Parents must act responsibly and accept that young children do not get the final say on *any* matters affecting their best interests.

Domestic violence

It goes without saying that violent or abusive conduct by a parent toward any child is going to be relevant in the assessment of that parent's custodial plan, because such behaviour clearly relates to one's parenting skills. When a child has been abused by a parent, it is often necessary to impose restrictions and limitations on the contact that may occur between the child and that parent. Sometimes the contact may only be in writing, such as birthday cards, letters, and e-mails, and sometimes visitation must occur in a supervised setting, such as a child protection agency or a community supervised access centre. In cases of severe abuse, the offending parent is almost always prohibited from having any contact whatsoever with the child.

A more complex question is the relevance and weight to be applied to violent and abusive conduct directed at a partner. If a parent has committed acts of domestic violence toward the other parent, to what extent should this conduct be considered in a custody and access dispute? Some people argue that a parent who has been violent or abusive toward the other parent is an unfit parent and should never have custody of his/her children. Others argue that if the misconduct was directed only at the other parent and not the children, it should be considered irrelevant because (1) it had nothing to do with the children and (2) in any event, the parents are now separated, so no further acts of violence or abuse are going to occur. Others will say that the relevance of partner abuse in custody and access cases depends on whether the children witnessed the violence or abuse.

In some jurisdictions, the law requires the court to take into account a parent's acts of domestic violence or abuse when assessing parenting capacity. I agree that such behaviour must be considered whether or not the children witnessed it. A parent who has been abusive or violent toward a partner may have problems with anger management or impulse control. A parent who has behaved this way with one partner may do so again with his/her next partner, to whom the children will probably be exposed. Children should not grow up believing that spousal violence and abuse are acceptable because they may imitate their parents in their own relationships. Children must be taught by example that violence and abuse are never acceptable. There is also a concern that a parent who loses his/her temper and acts violently toward a spouse may well do so toward a child during arguments and disagreements. For all these reasons, most courts will take into consideration any domestic violence that has occurred in the family, when deciding what is in a child's best interests.

Chapter 3 explained the purpose and importance of restraining orders when domestic violence has occurred. A spouse who has been victimized by the other spouse must have safeguards in place to protect him/her from further assaults or threats of violence. A restraining order will define the extent and form of communication and contact that the parents may have with each other. The parents may need to communicate through a third party, such as an adult family member or counsellor, or they may be restricted to communicating only in written form, such as a communication log or by e-mail. It is crucial that both parents in this situation strictly comply with the terms of the restraining order to prevent recurrences and further court proceedings arising from breaches of the order. The perpetrator may be required to participate in anger management counselling, and the victim may need to engage in counselling to help him/her overcome the emotional impact of the abuse. If the children have witnessed the spousal abuse, they may also need counselling to help them heal from any trauma they may have suffered.

The weight to be given to evidence of domestic violence in determining custody and access disputes depends on the specific circumstances of each case. Some people think that a parent who has committed even one act of abuse against the other parent should never again have contact with his/her children. I cannot agree that this should always be the case, as each family's situation is unique. As hard as this may be for some people to accept, the fact is that a person who has been abusive toward his/her partner *may* nevertheless be a good parent, especially once the parties are separated and the stress of living in an unhappy relationship is over. Obviously all of the circumstances must be examined, such as the nature of the parent-child relationship, the details and duration of the abuse, and the crucial issues of whether the children were involved and whether their independent views and preferences are ascertainable. The judge's task in custody cases is always the same: to decide what is in the best interests of the children, having regard to all of the circumstances. I certainly have seen cases in which a parent's abusive conduct toward the other parent resulted in a denial of contact with his/her child. But one thing is clear: there is no hard and fast rule prohibiting a parent who has committed partner abuse from having a relationship with his/her children. Each case must be decided on the basis of its particular facts.

Assessments

In some cases, the parents decide to jointly hire a psychiatrist, psychologist, or social worker to conduct an assessment of the child's needs and each parent's ability and willingness to meet those needs. Sometimes the judge will order an assessment even though neither party has requested it. Assessors are skilled, neutral professionals whose expertise can be very helpful in determining a child's best interests and developing the best possible parenting plan.

Unfortunately, assessments can be very costly and not many jurisdictions provide free services. I am fortunate to preside in a jurisdiction that has a government agency available to conduct a limited number of investigations by trained social workers who prepare reports for the parties and the court. These reports are not quite the same as assessments but do provide a great deal of background information about the family, and they make helpful custody and access recommendations.

Assessments can cause delay in a court case because they take at least several months to be completed. The assessor must spend many hours meeting with parents (with and without the children), and it may be necessary for the assessor to obtain additional information from family members, teachers, medical personnel, child protection workers, police officers, and other community sources. Then the assessor has to prepare a thorough report setting out his/her findings and recommendations, and possibly attend court to testify if there is a trial.

Assessments are available in the mediation, arbitration, and collaborative law processes. You do not need to have a court case to obtain an assessment. If you think your family could benefit from an assessment, this should be discussed with your lawyer.

Access by noncustodial parent

If one parent has been granted custody, the other parent (called the *noncustodial parent*) will usually be granted access (visitation) with the child. Many parents refer to their "access rights," but the law views access as the right of the *child*.[1] It is every child's fundamental right to enjoy a loving relationship with each parent, and it is every parent's obligation to ensure that this right is respected. Only in rare cases would it be appropriate for a child to have no contact whatsoever with a parent. A custodial parent should not attempt to suspend or terminate the other parent's access without being advised by a family law lawyer or child protection worker to do so.

As with custody cases, access decisions are made on the basis of the best interests of the child, and the same factors set out above will apply. Visitation schedules are highly individual matters that depend to a great extent on the history of the parent's involvement with the child and the degree of bonding and attachment that exists between them, given the child's age and level of development. Many other factors must also be considered, including the parents' work schedules, the children's routines and activities, the distance between the parents' homes, the availability of transportation to and from visits, and the children's wishes (if appropriate). Access can take the form of physical visits including overnight stays, or telephone calls, e-mails, letters, and even video conferencing when the parent and child are separated by a great distance. Special arrangements are often made for school vacation periods, religious holidays, and special occasions such as birthdays, Mother's Day, Father's Day, school events, and sports tournaments. Some parents even have detailed access arrangements for Halloween.

In the case of young infants, access may be limited to several hours at a time if breastfeeding and/or napping must be accommodated. Until a child is developmentally ready to be separated from his/her primary caregiver for extended periods, access might have to occur only during the day and not overnight. If the noncustodial parent has not had much contact with the child, then access must proceed gradually to make it a pleasant experience for the child, and to give the child an opportunity to develop an emotional bond with the parent. It is important to be patient with children, as each child has a unique personality and there is no fixed timetable dictating the creation of parent-child bonds. There are trained professionals, such as child psychologists and social workers, who can provide parents with advice and guidance in arriving at workable visitation schedules. There are also books and Web sites that contain excellent parenting plan suggestions and options.[2]

Sometimes access must occur in the presence of another adult (usually a mutually agreed-upon family member) or at a government- or community-operated supervised access centre, if it is in the child's best interests to do so. For example, an inexperienced parent who has little prior involvement with a young infant might start off by having supervised visits to help him/her learn basic childcare skills. Or if a noncustodial parent has a substance abuse or untreated mental health problem, or if for some reason the child is fearful of the parent, supervised access may be appropriate. In most cases supervised access is a temporary arrangement that assists children and noncustodial parents to develop the necessary comfort level and bonding with each other so access can eventually progress to become unsupervised.

The custodial parent has a responsibility to foster positive relationships between his/her children and the noncustodial parents. Children need emotional permission from the custodial parent to enjoy their access visits. This is done by speaking positively to the child about the other parent, and by encouraging access visits. Many young children are reluctant to go to access visits because they find it difficult to detach from their custodial parent, who is, after all, their primary caregiver. This is normal. These same children usually find it equally difficult to detach from their noncustodial parents at the end of the visits. Parents must be sensitive to their children's feelings and do all they can to make access visits a normal, happy part of their children's lives. If you have difficulties managing your children's behaviour or anxieties surrounding access visits, you are encouraged to consult your child's doctor or a child psychologist or social worker.

One very important aspect of access visits is the pickup and return of the child (called *access exchanges*). There is no general rule about where this is to be done; it depends on the circumstances in each case. Some parents are content to have the exchange of the children take place at the children's home. Others prefer to have the pickup and return occur at the children's school or daycare centre. Some parents agree to meet at a mall, restaurant, or subway station, or at the home of a relative or friend. The goal is to make these exchanges safe for everyone and free of conflict.

Parents should *never* use access exchanges to argue with each other or discuss adult issues in front of their children. You can be sure that your children watch and listen to what you say during access exchanges. Your children need to have the impression that you are both on the same team, working together to give them a secure and happy childhood — even if this is not true. Parents should love their children enough to put on an act and pretend to be friends with each other for these very brief interactions. Is this too much to ask? For your children's sake, no matter what, act maturely: be pleasant and civil with each other at all times in their presence. If you feel this is not possible, speak to your lawyer about having the access exchanges conducted through an intermediary, such as a relative or family friend. Some community access centres offer supervised exchange services in which the parents do not have to see each other. This is a good option if you do not have a relative or friend to help you out. I have even had cases in which the access exchanges occurred at a police station. What are children supposed to think about parents who require the presence of police officers just to facilitate access exchanges? While having access exchanges at a police station is hardly conducive to promoting a positive and nurturing environment for children, the sad reality for some families is there is no other alternative.

One final word about access visits. Some noncustodial parents use their children as spies. Instead of spending quality time engaging their children in fun activities, they quiz their children about the other parent's life (especially jobs, assets, and new partners). Similarly, some custodial parents interrogate their children upon their return from access visits to find out about the other parent's life. This is very unfair to children and can greatly distress them. Children in this situation quickly learn what kind of information will please or upset each parent. Some children come to the conclusion that the only way to survive is to keep silent about one parent when in the presence of the other. Others decide to make up lies to tell each parent about the other parent's life. Imagine how stressful this must be for a child who, after all, bears no blame for the parental animosity.

Another frequent problem is the use by parents of children as messengers. A great many parents make their children the intermediary in disputes regarding child support, payment of debts, and division of matrimonial property. This is sensitive information that children do not need to know, and it may upset them. Besides, I have seen more than my share of cases in which the child did not understand the message he/she was being asked to convey and did not communicate it accurately, causing unnecessary stress to all concerned. If you have information about financial, legal, or other adult matters to give the other parent, communicate by telephone, e-mail, fax, or letter. If you do not want to convey the message personally, then have your lawyer or a relative or friend do it. Remember, maturity is the name of the game.

---

1   In some jurisdictions, access is a joint right of the parent and child.

2   For a start, see the books listed in "Suggested Reading." See also: Child Custody Parenting Plan Options at **www.coloradodivorcemediation.com/family/parent_plans.asp**, Suggested Visitation Schedules at **www.emeryondivorce.com/parenting_plans.php**, and **www.coloradodivorcemediation.com/family/schedules.asp**.

CHAPTER SEVEN

JOINT CUSTODY:
IF PARENTS ARE EQUAL, WHY DO SO FEW HAVE IT?

THE TITLE OF THIS CHAPTER POSES THE MOST FREQUENTLY ASKED QUES-
TION I HEAR FROM PARENTS WHOSE CHILDREN DO NOT LIVE WITH THEM.
Virtually every parent in this situation wants joint custody, but in my
experience very few actually know what it means or how it would
work in their situations. I often get the impression that parents ask for
joint custody because they don't want the other parent to "win" the
court case. These people do not understand that a custody case is
about the best interests of the child, not the parents' egos. In this chapter I will explain the concept of joint custody and describe some
variations of it. If you are wondering whether you and your ex-partner are candidates for joint custody, this chapter should start you
thinking in the right direction.

What is joint custody?
Joint custody is the ideal parenting arrangement that all parents
should strive to attain if possible. It is premised upon the concept
that parents, working co-operatively, are most qualified to make decisions in their children's best interests. In some jurisdictions, the law
presumes that joint custody will apply in all cases unless the parent
who is opposing it can satisfy the court that joint custody would be

contrary to the child's best interests.

Parents who have joint custody have *equal decision-making powers* regarding their children. They make decisions together on the all-important issues of how their children's time will be divided between them, what schools they will attend, what religious training they will receive, how their healthcare needs will be met, and what extracurricular activities they will participate in. It is possible that parents who disagree on one or more issues (for example, access) can have joint custody, with the court deciding the issues in dispute. However, joint custody is generally intended for children whose parents do not need a judge to make decisions about their children. Ideally, parents with joint custody should also agree on how child support responsibilities will be divided between them, although strictly speaking this is a financial matter that would not necessarily stand in the way of joint custody being granted.

There are many misconceptions about joint custody. Some people think it means that a child's time must be split evenly between the parents. It could mean this, but only if the parents agree to this living arrangement. Parents with joint custody are free to agree to whatever shared parenting arrangement they want, just like parents who live together. In my experience, most parents with joint custody agree that a child will have a primary residence with one parent and spend a lot of time with the other parent. However, joint custody is not defined by how much time a child spends with each parent; it is defined by *how the decisions are made.*

Some people think joint custody means that each parent "gets a say" in major decisions affecting the child. You don't need to have joint custody to have the right to be consulted before important decisions are made about your child. Nor do you need joint custody to be entitled to receive the same information about your child as the custodial parent receives from schools, doctors, and other service providers. These rights can be given to you in a court order.

Joint custody is all about the way decisions are made. Parents with joint custody are required to make decisions together as co-parents. They must be able to communicate and co-operate with each other in a calm, civilized, mature way. They do not have to be best friends — perfect co-operation is not expected — but it certainly helps if they can at least be friendly with each other. If your relationship with your ex-partner since separation does not meet these requirements, it is unlikely that joint custody would be granted.

Most people I see in family court are not candidates for joint custody. Let's face it: if they could reach agreements with each other, they wouldn't be in court. Although the fact of being in court will not prevent a parent from asking for, and possibly getting, joint custody, it will not likely be granted unless the court is satisfied that the parents can communicate effectively. I have had parents ask for joint custody even though they have been convicted of assaulting the other parent and are bound by a no-contact term in a probation order! I have had parents ask for joint custody even though they haven't communicated with the other parent for years, except in a courtroom. I have had parents ask for joint custody even though they do not have the other parent's address or telephone number. And believe it or not, I have had parents ask for joint custody even though they have told me they never again want to see or speak to the other parent! How in the world do these people think that joint custody would work?

I remember one case in which the parents of a young child had agreed to joint custody without first getting legal advice. Soon afterwards, the problems began and the parents could not agree on anything. One day, the child was hit by a car and taken to hospital by ambulance. When both parents arrived at the hospital, they immediately began arguing and fighting with each other. Because they had joint custody, they both had to sign surgical consents, but they were too busy fighting with each other to focus on what the doctors were trying to tell them. In desperation, the hospital called the local child protection agency, who obtained an emergency court order in order to make the child a temporary ward so that the necessary consent for treatment could be provided. This is an example of what can happen when parents with joint custody cannot communicate and co-operate with each other.

A claim for joint custody should be made only on the advice of a family law lawyer. Your lawyer can assess your situation and advise you realistically whether joint custody is an option in your case. If you are a parent who has received a request from the other parent for joint custody, you also need to consult a lawyer about whether joint custody would be appropriate in your situation.

Sometimes parents start out angry and hostile toward each other during the immediate post-separation period and then move beyond their acrimony after several months or even years. Many parents benefit enormously through counselling and eventually are able to develop a good mutual working relationship for the sake of their children. I have seen many cases in which joint custody, though initially inappropriate, was granted after the parents made the necessary adjustments to their attitudes and behaviour. This is certainly to be encouraged, as joint custody, with parents working together as a decision-making team, is the ideal that all parents should strive to attain if possible.

Parallel parenting

In recent years, the concept of parallel parenting has been developed to accommodate the greatest possible flexibility in child custody law. It has evolved from the notion that there are essentially two aspects of child custody: (1) the right to have the child in your physical care and (2) the right to make decisions about the child. Traditionally, these two rights have been given to one person — the person having custody of the child. That is, the child resides with the custodial parent (except during specified times when the other parent has access), and that parent makes all decisions for the child. However, it is possible to unbundle these aspects of custody and divide them between the parents in appropriate cases.

Here are just a few examples of parallel parenting arrangements. The child could live with Parent A but have all school decisions made by Parent B. The child might live with Parent B but have all healthcare decisions made by Parent A. The child might live with Parent A but all decisions regarding extracurricular activities might be made by Parent B. The child might live with Parent B but Parent A might be in charge of the child's religious upbringing. The child might live with Parent A and Parent B on alternate weeks, with each parent making decisions during the times the child is with him/her. Parent A and Parent B might have apartments in the same building, with the child essentially living in two homes on a flexible shared custody basis with no fixed schedule, and the parents might agree to divide the decision-making functions as needed from time to time. There is no end of possibilities; it all depends on the needs of the children and the creativity of the parents in meeting those needs. I even had one case where the child lived with Parent A, but Parent B had the exclusive right to decide when and where the child would get haircuts!

Why would it ever be a good thing to split up the decision-making functions for a child? Some parents with special expertise in certain areas think their children benefit most by having decisions in those areas made by them, even if the children do not live with them and even if they are not responsible for making other major decisions. For example, many doctors want to be in charge of their children's medical care. Many teachers want to be in charge of their children's education. In families in which one parent has strong religious beliefs and the other does not, it is not uncommon for the parent with strong religious beliefs to be responsible for the child's religious training.

The difference between joint custody and parallel parenting is that in joint custody, the parents are expected to make all major decisions together, whereas in parallel parenting, each parent is given the right to make decisions about specific matters. Parallel parenting may not require the same high level of communication and co-operation between the parents as joint custody. Some courts have ruled that parallel parenting arrangements may be acceptable even if parents have difficulty communicating or reaching a consensus on the child's upbringing. However, even if this is true, there can be no doubt that parallel parenting works best when parents get along well with each other. Children need stability and consistency in all aspects of their lives. They cannot have parents making contradictory decisions for them or arguing over the correctness of each other's decisions. If parents cannot be reasonable with each other and respect each other's decisions, parallel parenting is not advisable.

I have seen cases in which parents were in dispute over the scope of each other's authority because they could not agree on what constituted healthcare, education, religion, or extracurricular activities. In one case, Parent A was given the right to make healthcare decisions and Parent B engaged the child in counselling. Parent A argued that counselling was part of healthcare and therefore Parent B did not have the right to take the child to counselling. Parent B argued that healthcare decisions involved only medical care from doctors, not therapy given by psychologists. In another case, Parent A was responsible for the child's education and Parent B enrolled the child in piano lessons as an extracurricular activity. Parent A took the position that Parent B had no authority to do this, as piano lessons form part of a child's education, since one has to learn to play the piano. Some parents cannot agree on whether Sunday school at church is within the realm of education or religion. As you can see, some activities do not fit neatly into one category, and there can be some overlap. Parallel parenting is premised on the parents being reasonable with each other. In the wrong hands, parallel parenting can set parents up for years of endless power struggles in which each parent challenges the other's authority and judgment.

If you are interested in exploring the possibilities that parallel parenting has to offer, consult a family law lawyer. If you and your ex-partner are candidates for joint custody or parallel parenting, you probably will not need to go to court to arrive at a parenting plan. Your lawyer may advise you to engage in mediation or the collaborative law process discussed in Chapter 4.

A message to parents who are not candidates for joint custody

Every day I see noncustodial parents who are devastated to learn they are not candidates for joint custody. They want to get along with the custodial parent and feel that he/she is deliberately refusing to be co-operative in order to obtain and retain sole custody. For all I know, this could very well be true. How is a judge to know what really motivates people, or why two people are not able to communicate and co-operate with each other? The problem may rest with one or both parties. Almost every litigant in family court feels like a victim and believes the other party is more responsible than him/herself for the problems that brought them to court. This is normal. As Anaïs Nin wrote, "We do not see things as they are; we see things as *we* are." Each parent has his/her own unique and highly subjective perspective of what has transpired in the relationship.

Unfortunately, no one, not even a judge, can make two people get along if they don't want to. If one person does not want to communicate with the other, what difference does it make what that person's reasons are? The fact remains that the parties are not likely to make decisions together in a civilized and mature way, and the child may suffer as a result. Children need decisions to be made for their well-being every day. They cannot languish in legal limbo in the hopes that their parents may one day come to their senses and start working as a team. Life goes on for children whether or not their parents get along with each other.

Some people advocate that joint custody should be ordered even when parents do not get along. They argue that parents must get a clear message from the court that they are equally important and that they have an obligation to put aside their differences and work as a team for the benefit of their children. They also make the important point that children need to know that neither parent is more important than the other, and that this message can best be conveyed by a joint custody order. They urge judges not to reward unreasonable parents by granting them sole custody just because they refuse to deal with the other parent for no good reason.

There is much to be said for these arguments, and judges struggle with this dilemma every day. A parent should not be permitted to use his/her own refusal to communicate with the other parent as a reason to oppose joint custody. It is absolutely correct that people who behave unreasonably should not be given the impression that they are being rewarded for their misconduct. On the other hand, family courts are not in the business of rewarding or punishing anyone, even though there is often a "win-lose" mentality among litigants — and unfortunately, even among some misguided lawyers. Everyone should be mindful that there are no "winners" in family court when the fighting continues — *everyone* loses, especially the children.

Custody cases are concerned with the best interests of children, not the best interests of parents. If after conducting a best-interests analysis (see Chapter 6) a court concludes that a parent should have custody even though he/she has not tried hard enough to get along with the other parent, this is not being done to reward or punish anyone. It is being done because it is in the child's best interests to be in that parent's custody *despite* his/her faults. Custody orders are made on the basis of the best parenting arrangement for the child in the circumstances of the case — not the best parenting arrangement in an ideal world.

You have to accept that no court order is going to change your ex-partner's personality or your own. Court orders are made by judges, not magicians. Judges make orders in the hopes of affecting behaviour and parental attitudes. We spend many hours in court trying to convince parents to treat each other with maturity and respect; in fact, that is why I have written this book. But the fact remains that people are who they are, and custodial arrangements for children must be realistic and practical given the dynamic between the parents.

This means that if you and your ex-partner do not get along well enough to make decisions together, it is not likely that joint custody will be granted. I am not necessarily saying that you each do not *deserve* to have an equal say in the child's upbringing; I am saying that *together as co-parents* you may not be candidates for this arrangement.

There have been cases in which courts made joint custody orders against the wishes of one parent. Those cases generally fall into three categories: (1) the judge was satisfied that the parents had already demonstrated a track record of sufficiently co-operative decision making since separation; (2) the judge was satisfied that the parents would be able to do so in the future; or (3) the parents were mostly in agreement with each other about the major issues affecting the child, and only a few issues (for example, access) had to be decided by the court. Sometimes a judge concludes that the parties' adversarial relationship is mostly being fuelled by the court case itself, and that their animosity will come to an end when the litigation ends, making joint custody feasible. There have even been some cases in which joint custody was ordered in response to one parent's totally unreasonable refusal to communicate with the other parent. However, as a general rule, a court will not impose joint custody on an unwilling parent unless it is satisfied that both parents have the necessary maturity and child-focused attitudes to rise above their differences and work together as co-parents.

Even if joint custody is not appropriate in your case, there are two important rights noncustodial parents can request:

1) The right to be consulted in writing by the custodial parent at least sixty days (or as much as possible) in advance of making any major decision for the child (except in emergencies). In this way, if a custodial parent is contemplating changing the child's residence, school, religion, name, healthcare, or extracurricular activities, the noncustodial parent will receive advance notice and can take court action if necessary. If the custodial parent makes the change without obeying the notice requirement, the noncustodial parent may be able to take court action depending on the law in your jurisdiction.

2) The right to receive the same information as the custodial

parent receives about the child from schools, doctors, and other services providers. This enables the noncustodial parent to obtain copies of report cards, invitations to parent-teacher interviews and other school events, and medical reports directly rather than having to rely on the custodial parent to provide them.

There may be other specific rights that a noncustodial parent might request, such as the right to be notified if the child is being removed from the country, or the right to receive copies of certain documents such as health cards or birth certificates. In my experience, many custodial parents are willing to consent to the above terms. This should be discussed with your lawyer.

There is an emotional factor that figures prominently in custody cases and yet is rarely mentioned: fear. Many custodial parents are afraid of being controlled by their ex-partners and interpret requests for joint custody as attempts to dominate them. Many noncustodial parents ask for joint custody primarily because they are afraid of somehow becoming "second-class parents." Even if joint custody is not appropriate in your case, there are effective ways to address these fears. Every day lawyers help parents negotiate custody and access arrangements that allow them to be independent and to get on with their lives, while at the same time remaining actively involved in their children's lives.

If you are a noncustodial parent whose claim for joint custody has been denied, please remember that to your child, "custody" is just a word. For that matter, the word "parent" is a *verb* as well as a noun — it's what you do that matters to your child, not what your court order says. You do not need to have custody or joint custody to be an involved and active parent, and you are not second best just because your custody claim was denied. Put your ego aside and concentrate on playing an important role in your child's life; your child deserves nothing less and will thank you for it one day.

Call it what you will — it's all about maturity

One final word to those interested in the topic of joint custody. Some experts have suggested doing away with legal terms such as *custody* and *access* altogether. They suggest we refer instead to *parenting time* or *residency* and create *equal time* or *maximum contact* presumptions to encourage parents to treat each other as equals. These are interesting possibilities worth exploring. Sometimes the language we use can be an emotional lightning rod and an obstacle to achieving compromise. Whatever wording is used, the major prerequisite for responsible post-separation parenting remains the same: maturity. Any initiative that will help instill a child-focused approach to parenting rights and responsibilities is worth considering. Positive steps that will maximize the role of every parent in each child's life are always welcome. We must do all we can to reinforce the message to separated parents that they should respect each other's roles in their children's lives.

Joint custody and child support

It is well known that a noncustodial parent must pay child support to the custodial parent. What about parents granted joint custody? Some parents with joint custody are surprised to learn that they are still required to pay child support. This is because they confuse the decision-making aspects of joint custody with the issue of how the child's material needs are to be met. In the typical joint custody scenario, where the child's primary residence is with Parent A and the child spends a lot of time with Parent B, it is likely that Parent B will be required to pay child support in the same way as if Parent A had been granted sole custody. This is because in most joint custody situations, the fact that parents are making decisions together does not change the way in which the child's expenses are being financed.

Obviously, the amount of time a child spends with each parent is an important consideration in assessing child support obligations. An equally important consideration is the disparity, if any, in the parents' incomes. As a general rule, a child's lifestyle should be relatively consistent in each parent's home. If one parent's income is much higher than the other's, it would not be appropriate for the child to live in luxury with one parent and in poverty with the other. This is why some parents who have the child even as much as 50 per cent of the time (and maybe more) are still required to pay child support to the other parent.

I have had cases in which a parent's only reason for requesting joint custody or more access time was because of a mistaken belief that this would reduce his/her child support. Of course, decisions regarding the best interests of children should never be motivated by financial considerations. You should not assume that because you have joint custody or some other form of shared parenting arrangement, your child support obligations will necessarily be affected. The law governing child support differs from jurisdiction to jurisdiction, and it is necessary to consult a family law lawyer to advise you on how the law affects your particular circumstances. (For more information regarding the relationship between access and child support, see Chapter 9.)

CHAPTER EIGHT

PATERNITY AND CHILD SUPPORT

PARENTS ARE REQUIRED BY LAW TO SUPPORT THEIR CHILDREN. Child support payments are made by noncustodial parents to custodial parents. The amount to be paid depends on the annual income of the payor and the number of children being supported. There are government-enacted child support guidelines in most jurisdictions, setting out charts (called *tables*) that make it easy to calculate the amount of support to be paid in any given situation. This is called the *table amount*. In addition to the table amount, there may be special expenses such as daycare, medical or dental fees, summer camp, and fees for extracurricular activities that must be paid. These additional expenses are usually shared between the parents in proportion to their incomes.

Depending on the law where you live, the amount of child support can be adjusted in certain situations. For example, a parent who has the child in his/her care a great deal of time may be able to pay a reduced amount. A parent who spends a lot of money in travel costs for access purposes may be permitted to pay reduced child support. (These two situations are discussed in Chapter 9.) There may be other circumstances justifying an adjustment, upward or downward, to the amount of child support that must be paid. The rules dealing with the support of adult dependant children who are full time students may in some places be different than the rules dealing with minor children (see Chapter 12). In many jurisdictions, the law allows the court to exercise some discretion to reduce the amount of child support if the payor can establish that he/she would suffer undue hardship[1] by being required to pay the table amount. For specific advice about your own situation, you are well advised to consult a family law lawyer.

Parents must support their children

Although there are differences between jurisdictions in the law governing how child support is calculated, one thing is true everywhere: parents are required to support their children.[2] It's a matter of DNA: if a paternity test proves you are a child's biological parent, you must support that child. It doesn't matter whether you and the other parent were married or even lived together. Even a child who was the product of a very casual intimate encounter has the same right as every other child to be financially supported by his/her parents.

Some of the most interesting family court cases have been about the determination of paternity in connection with child support obligations. There is a never-ending list of inventive reasons that some people have come up with, hoping to avoid paying support for their biological children. I once had a man tell me that he shouldn't have to pay child support because, "I only slept with the child's mother once and I didn't enjoy it." Another parent, who was the child's biological father, had undergone sex reassignment surgery and argued that she was now a mother, not a father, and therefore her child support obligation should end! You can guess the result in both cases.

There have also been many cases in which the father alleged that he was "tricked" by the mother into having unprotected sex. For example, if a woman told a man she was using birth control, would he have to pay child support if she lied about it? The answer in most jurisdictions is yes. Biological parents have to support their children regardless of how they were conceived, because child support is the right of the child. I remember one amusing case involving a man who claimed he should not have to pay child support because, "when the condom broke, she fixed it with chewing gum and assured me that it would keep her from getting pregnant." The moral of the story is — well, you can figure that one out for yourself.

In one extremely unusual case, a female college student asked a male friend for a sample of his sperm "for a school science project." She then inseminated herself with the sperm, and nine months later a child was born. The man was stunned to find himself responding to an application for child support in family court. Although he had clearly been the victim of a trick, he was the child's biological father and was obliged to pay child support. So consider yourself warned: if you are a child's biological parent, it is highly likely that you will be responsible to support the child regardless of the circumstances surrounding conception.

Paternity testing

When a man receives an application for child support and responds by denying or questioning his paternity (sometimes called *filiation*), the court can order DNA testing if there is some basis to question paternity. The man, the child's mother, and the child will have to go to a laboratory that conducts paternity tests (they can go at separate times if they wish). Most laboratories conduct the test in a painless and non-intrusive way by swabbing the inside of the mouth with a cotton swab, to get DNA from the saliva. The science of DNA has developed to the point that paternity can be established (or excluded) with virtual certainty.

As a general rule, the court will decide who pays for the paternity test by considering all the circumstances, including the level of doubt about paternity that has been raised by the evidence and the parties' financial means. Regardless of who pays for the test, one thing is clear: if the man is found not to be the father, the court will almost always order the mother to reimburse him for expenses he incurred in the court case.

What happens if DNA testing is ordered and one of the parties refuses to be tested? In most jurisdictions, such behaviour will count against that person. If the mother refuses (or doesn't bring the child), the court may assume that she didn't want to risk being wrong, and her child support application will likely be dismissed. If the man refuses to be tested, the court may assume that this was because he did not want to have his paternity confirmed. This is sometimes referred to as *the court drawing a negative inference* and can lead to a finding of paternity being made against the man who refused to be tested. If you have been ordered by a court to have a paternity test, you should definitely do it unless a lawyer advises you not to and brings the proper motion to set aside the order for testing.

I remember one case in which the man did not want to submit to paternity testing because he was married to a woman who was unaware of his extramarital affair with the child's mother. He argued that his privacy rights would be violated if he had to submit to a paternity test, and that his marriage would be jeopardized if his wife were to learn about his extramarital affair. Unfortunately for persons in his situation, children's rights come first. Parents are required to financially support their children regardless of any embarrassment this may cause.

I rejected the father's privacy argument because in the jurisdiction where I preside, all family court files dealing with child support are public records and therefore he had already lost his privacy when the mother started her court application.[3] Besides, in appropriate cases the court has the discretion to seal the court file (make it closed to the public), so this was not a good reason to deny paternity testing. Given the clear evidence that the man could very well be the father (he had admitted to the affair), I ordered paternity testing. The test conclusively proved that he was indeed the child's father. Not surprisingly, the mother agreed to withdraw the court application and a private agreement dealing with custody, access, and child support was reached.

In another unusual case, a mother brought a child support application against two men. She claimed that she had a relationship with both men at the same time and that she had no idea which one was the father. She was requesting paternity testing for both men. Neither man knew of the other's existence. I found it amusing that the men, who were each married, were more upset about the woman's "infidelity" than about the prospect of paying child support! To my amazement, the paternity test results showed that *neither* man was the child's father. When I questioned the mother about how this could possibly be the case, she sheepishly recalled a third man who had briefly been in her life during the relevant time but whom she had forgotten about. As you might expect, I ordered her to pay full legal costs (including the costs of the DNA tests) to the two men she had sued for support. She never appeared in my courtroom again, so I do not know if she pursued the third man for child support.

Don't delay

If you have been served with an application for child support, and you have reason to believe that you may not be the child's father, it is very important to raise the paternity issue right away. For some reason, a lot of men do not question the child's paternity when child support is first requested, and then decide to do so many years later. This can be problematic. In many American states, a parent who waits too long to question paternity can be prevented by the *doctrine of equitable estoppel* from getting a DNA test or denying paternity. Even in jurisdictions where it is possible to raise the issue of paternity after a long delay, most courts will expect a reasonable explanation for the delay. For example, I have had cases in which several years after child support was ordered, the payor and the child's mother had an argument during which she told him that he was not the child's father. I have also had cases where, long after child support was ordered, the payor obtained a copy of the child's birth registration documents and found that the mother had written "unknown" where the father's name should have been given. I have even had cases in which the birth registration documents showed someone else's name as the father. In each of these cases, I ordered paternity testing because the support payor had raised genuine doubt about the child's paternity, and there are important reasons for knowing the truth.

Delay in settling paternity questions can cause practical problems. I once had a case in which child support had been paid for many years without problems. When the child was nineteen years old, the mother brought a motion to increase the child support to include a contribution toward the child's college expenses. The payor responded by denying paternity and asking for DNA testing. He claimed that he had recently acquired some information about the mother's past that led him to seriously question whether he was the child's father. The mother insisted that the payor was the father, but said she would be happy to go for paternity testing if it would put the payor's mind at ease. I made the order for paternity testing, and two months later the parties were back before me with no test results. Both parties had gone to the lab and submitted DNA samples, but the nineteen-year-old child refused to go. He said he was deeply offended that his father would at this late stage question paternity, and he felt sure his father's real motivation was a desire to stop paying child support.

This was a real dilemma. The father argued the child support should be terminated because of the child's refusal to be tested. The mother said that she had tried to get her son to go for testing, but that she couldn't force him, as he was legally an adult. She argued she should not be penalized because of her son's hurt feelings, and that without a financial contribution from the father, she would not be able to pay for her son's college education. Aside from having to decide the legal question of whether the court had authority to make the son (who was not a party in the case) go for testing, I was distressed that the father's delay in raising the paternity issue had seriously damaged the father-son relationship. I ended up deciding that, even if the court had jurisdiction to order the adult son to submit to a paternity test, this was not an appropriate case to make such an order. The father's reasons for questioning paternity at this late stage were too weak and speculative to impose any further stress on the son.

There is another reason not to delay if you have doubt about paternity. What happens if, after child support has been paid for many years, a paternity test[4] establishes that the payor is not the child's father? Can the payor get his money back? The answer depends on the law where you live. Only some jurisdictions allow the court to order the mother to reimburse the father for all support funds paid to her. In other jurisdictions, no reimbursement can be ordered by the family court, and the payor is left with the uncertain option of suing the recipient on the basis of fraud, duress, mistake of fact, or negligence. This can be quite a challenge if the payor did not question paternity when the support order was first made. All of this can be avoided by dealing with the issue of paternity as soon as possible. If you have reason to believe that you may not be the father of a child you are being asked to support (or are already supporting), it is imperative that you consult a family law lawyer right away. Don't wait until it may be too late to be reimbursed if it turns out that your doubt was justified.

My comments about delay apply equally to mothers. I have had cases in which a child was the result of a casual short-term relationship, and the mother chose not to tell the father he had a child. Then, when the child was an adolescent, the mother decided to apply for child support and told the father he had a child. Imagine how shocking and upsetting it can be to learn, so long after a child's birth, that you are that child's parent — and more importantly, to have been deprived for so long of the chance to have a relationship with your child.

Despite the mother's delay, the law in most jurisdictions would require child support to be paid because it is the child's right to be supported. However, the mother's delay might be a serious factor in deciding the commencement date for support payments. Should the father have to pay retroactive child support going back to the date of the child's birth when he was not even aware he had a child? Would it be more fair to make child support payments start from the date the father was told he had a child? Should the payments start from the date the mother commenced her court action? Should they start from the date the father was served with the court papers? These are difficult questions that depend on the law where you live and on all of the circumstances, especially the mother's reasons for waiting so long to inform the father. Unless she has a reasonable explanation for the delay, she may find a court unwilling to impose a retroactive child support obligation on the father. (For more information about retroactive child support, see Chapter 12.)

Step-parents

In many jurisdictions a person can be required to pay child support even if he/she is not the child's biological parent. If you enter into a relationship with a person who already has a child and you treat that child as your own, you may be obliged to support that child just as if you were a biological parent. A step-parent in this situation is sometimes referred to as being *in loco parentis*. It is possible for a step-parent to be required to pay child support even if the child's biological parent is already paying child support. I have seen cases in which up to four different step-parents were paying child support for the same child, in addition to the child's biological parent; custodial parents in those cases could potentially receive more money than they would receive from one ex-partner.

If you start a relationship with a person who already has a child, would the law uphold an agreement stating that you will not have to support that child if you break up? In most jurisdictions the answer is no. You cannot agree to call an apple an orange. In other words, the court will closely examine the nature of your relationship with the child. If the court concludes that you treated your partner's child as your own during the relationship, you will likely be required to support the child regardless of the agreement you entered into when the relationship started.

In assessing child support to be paid by nonbiological parents, the court is usually permitted to deviate from the standard child support table amount and order a lower amount. All of the circumstances must be considered, including the length of the step-parent relationship, the incomes of the parties, the step-parent's other family support obligations, any special needs the child may have, and the amount of support being paid by the biological parent or any other step-parent. Not all jurisdictions impose child support obligations on step-parents. If you have questions about this, consult a family law lawyer to find out what the law has to say in your area.

Finding out you're not the father

What if you thought you were the father and it turns out you aren't? In one memorable case, a happily married man who believed he was the father of two adolescent children learned as a result of medical tests that he was sterile. When he confronted his wife with this information, she confessed to having had a long-standing affair with another man. Their marriage ended. The mother obtained an order for child support against the children's biological father. In addition, she applied for child support from her ex-husband, who had lived with, loved, and helped care for the children for their entire lives until the date of separation.

The ex-husband argued that, as he was not the biological father, he could only be held responsible to pay child support if he was a step-parent (in other words, if he had known the children were not his but decided to treat them as if they were). He argued that he could not make a decision to treat the children as if they were his own unless he first *knew* that they were not his own. There is a difference between (1) treating a child as your own because you know that the child *is* your own; and (2) treating a child as your own even though you know that he/she is *not* your own. In essence, the ex-husband took the position that it would be unfair to order a nonbiological parent to pay child support for a child that he/she believed to be his/her own.

As you can imagine, this is a very complex legal and moral issue. On the one hand, children have a right to be supported by their parents, and there was no question that the ex-husband was in every sense (except biological) a parent to these children — in fact, he was the only father these children had ever known. The children were completely innocent and had done nothing to deserve having their father stop supporting them. On the other hand, the father made an intriguing point: you cannot decide to treat someone else's child as your own if you don't know that the child is someone else's child. Besides, these children were now being supported by their biological father.

In American jurisdictions where the *doctrine of equitable estoppel* applies, the ex-husband would have been required to continue to support the children, because he had been a parent to them in every sense of the word and their right to continued support from him would be paramount. In many other jurisdictions, the doctrine is not necessarily applicable. In this particular case, the father was ordered to pay child support but in a lower amount than if he were the biological father (remember that the biological father was paying the full table amount). Other cases with similar facts have had opposite results. This is because the law remains unclear on what should happen in this situation. Some courts have ruled that a person in the ex-husband's situation must pay child support because he treated the children as his own, and the fact that he didn't know their true paternity is irrelevant. Other courts have ruled that a nonbiological parent does not have to support a child that he treated as his own if he was deprived of the necessary information about paternity to make an informed choice. Eventually this issue will have to be definitively resolved by either legislation or higher court rulings.

1   Undue hardship is a legal term found in the Canadian Child Support Guidelines. It sets out a rigorous legal test that, if satisfied, can permit a court to reduce the amount of child support to be paid. Circumstances giving rise to undue hardship include unusually high debts or access expenses and other family support obligations. A claim for undue hardship can succeed only if the payor's household standard of living is lower than that in the recipient's household. Some other jurisdictions provide a comparable legal test permitting the court to reduce child support in specific circumstances. For specific information about the law in your jurisdiction, consult a family law lawyer.

2   There are some exceptions: (1) If a parent can establish a total inability to pay, child support may not be ordered; (2) Some parents enter into agreements providing that no child support will be paid. These agreements will be binding unless a court rules otherwise; (3) If parental rights are terminated by adoption or because a child has become a ward of the state, the parent's child support obligation will terminate.

3   In many American jurisdictions, family court records are confidential, so this issue would not arise.

4   In many American jurisdictions, the results of privately arranged paternity tests are inadmissible. Only paternity testing conducted at state-approved laboratories pursuant to court orders is admissible.

CHAPTER NINE

THE "CONNECTION" BETWEEN ACCESS AND CHILD SUPPORT

THERE ARE MANY MYTHS SURROUNDING THE LEGAL RELATION-SHIP BETWEEN ACCESS AND CHILD SUPPORT. Some people believe that the amount of child support to be paid should depend on the amount of time the child spends with each parent. Some people believe that a parent who does not pay child support should have no access to the child. Some people believe that a support payor who is denied access to his/her children should not have to pay any child support. None of these statements is accurate. As a general rule in most jurisdictions, child support and access are separate matters, but there are some specific circumstances when there can be a connection for limited purposes. This chapter will explore those situations. Keep in mind that each jurisdiction may have different laws relating to the ways in which access and child support can interrelate. It is important to consult a family law lawyer and obtain legal advice about your own situation.

Access affecting amount of child support

Child spending a lot of time with noncustodial parent

As you know from Chapter 8, the law in most jurisdictions states that the amount of child support a noncustodial parent must pay depends on his/her annual income and the number of children being supported. There are government-enacted child support guidelines setting out charts (called *tables*) that make it easy to calculate the amount of support to be paid in any given situation. This is called the *table amount*. However, some jurisdictions provide that if a child is in the care of the noncustodial parent for a substantial amount of time, the child support payable by that parent may be less than the table amount. For example, in the jurisdiction where I preside, a noncustodial parent who has the child in his/her care at least 40 per cent of the time may be entitled to pay less than the table amount.

It is unfortunate that some parents engage in bitter disputes over custody and access in the hopes that the amount of child support will be affected to their advantage. As mentioned in Chapter 7, some noncustodial parents ask for joint custody, thinking this will lower or eliminate their child support payments. This is misguided, as joint custody has to do with *decision making* for children, not necessarily the amount of time each parent spends with the children. Some noncustodial parents launch major battles to increase the hours and minutes they can spend with their children just so they can reduce their child support. Conversely, some custodial parents vigorously resist the other parent's request for shared custody, or try to restrict the other parent's access, so that the amount of child support won't be reduced. In both situations this is inappropriate. The decision of how much time a child should spend with the noncustodial parent should be made in accordance with the child's best interests, not financial considerations. (For more information on how a child's best interests are determined, see Chapter 6.)

If a child spends a great deal of time in the support payor's care, this will not necessarily lead to a reduction in child support. In most jurisdictions, the support payor will have to show actual financial consequences in the form of increased expenses stemming from the shared custody arrangement. All noncustodial parents spend money on their children during access — they feed them, take them places, and buy them things. This will not generally be enough to justify a reduction in child support. All of the financial circumstances must be considered, including the budgets and actual expenditures by each parent in relation to their respective incomes. This is because children should not be exposed to a big discrepancy in living standards between one parent's household and the other's. If the discrepancy between the two homes is too great, this might jeopardize the shared parenting arrangement. This is why some parents who have their children with them a great deal of the time may still be required to pay the regular amount of child support. If you are wondering whether the amount of child support you are paying should be reduced because of a shared parenting arrangement, consult a family law lawyer.

Access not being exercised

What if no access is occurring? Can a custodial parent ask for an *increase* in the amount of child support over the table amount? I once had a case in which such a claim was made. The parents had joint custody, with Parent A having primary residence, and the child was to spend every weekend and weeknight with Parent B. Parent B was to pay the table amount of child support. Soon after the court order was made, Parent B entered into a new relationship, had a baby, and moved to a town three hours away. Parent B chose to see the child only one weekend per month. Parent A applied to increase the child support over the table amount. Parent A argued that, because the child was with Parent A much more than the court order stated, Parent A was spending a lot more money on the child than they would have if Parent B took the child according to the court-ordered access schedule.

Parent A's lawyer made an interesting point: if a support payor can in certain situations pay *less* child support because he/she spends a lot of time with the child, why shouldn't the support payor pay *more* child support when he/she chooses to spend little or no time with the child? Although I could certainly understand this reasoning, I could not increase the amount of support payable by Parent B because the law where I preside did not favour Parent A's claim. But who knows? The law is always developing to reflect societal values, and one cannot predict possible future parental rights and obligations. However, this issue is a slippery slope; if the law were to allow custodial parents to get increased child support if access is not happening, some unscrupulous custodial parents might be induced to deny access in the faint hope that they might get more money. This would certainly not be in the best interests of children.

What about the opposite situation? Can a noncustodial parent pay less or no child support if he/she agrees to have no access to the child? Some parents enter into agreements in these terms and abide by them. However, if after entering into such an agreement, a parent asks a court to overturn or change it, the court in most jurisdictions will not be bound by the agreement. As child support and access are separate legal matters — and, more importantly, as they are both rights of the *child* that cannot be bargained away by parents — the court will decide these issues according to the law. That is, child support will be determined by the applicable child support laws, and a request for access will be adjudicated in terms of the child's best interests.

I once had a case in which a noncustodial parent offered to have no access to the child in return for paying no child support. When it was explained that child support would still have to be paid even if access didn't occur, the parent asked for custody of the child. There is never a dull moment in family court.

Travel expenses

What if a noncustodial parent lives a great distance away from the child? The law in some places offers a limited possibility for a reduction in child support to help offset access travel expenses. However, the law is very complex and requires support payors to satisfy several difficult requirements before a reduction in child support can be granted. All of the circumstances must be considered, including the reason why the parties live such a great distance from each other (which parent moved away), the frequency of access visits, the transportation costs, and the parents' incomes and standards of living. If you are a noncustodial parent who spends an extraordinary amount of money on transportation costs for access visits, consult a family law lawyer. Your lawyer will review all of the circumstances and advise you whether you have a possible claim for a reduction in child support. Even if the law where you live does not permit the court to reduce child support to offset visitation expenses, the court will probably be able to deal with the payment of travel expenses as part of the access order.

Access and child support are not weapons

One of the biggest misconceptions among separated parents is that child support and access can be used as weapons of enforcement. That is, many custodial parents believe that if the noncustodial parent does not pay child support on time and in full every month, they are entitled to stop him/her from seeing the child. Conversely, many noncustodial parents believe that if they are denied access to their children, they are not required to pay child support. These misconceptions are so widespread that family court judges routinely spend hours explaining to parents that they are mistaken.

In most jurisdictions, child support and access are two separate matters. This is because access and child support are rights of the *child*, not rights of the parents. Every child has the right to be financially supported by both parents, and every child has the right to enjoy a relationship with both parents. If the child is being denied one of these rights, it is not fair to deny the child the other right. Two wrongs don't make a right. Parents should never use child support and access as weapons against each other because this only punishes the children.

Even if you are not receiving adequate child support from the non-custodial parent, your child has the right to have a relationship with that parent. In fact, your child would have this right even if the noncustodial parent could not afford to pay *any* child support. Child support should not be treated as payment for visitation rights. Access by parents to their children is not a financial issue. The decision of whether and to what extent a parent may have contact with his/her child is based on the best interests of the child, not the parent's bank account.

In most jurisdictions, child support is collected and enforced by government agencies, which have a wide variety of enforcement tools available to ensure that child support is paid (see Chapter 12). I am not aware of any jurisdiction that allows an enforcement agency or court to suspend or terminate a delinquent support payor's access as a means of enforcing child support. Nor am I aware of any case in which a court allowed a custodial parent to cut off access for the sole reason that child support was not being paid.

If you are a custodial parent in the unfortunate position of not receiving the child support owing to you, do not obstruct the other parent's access rights as a means of trying to induce payment. It cannot help a child who is being deprived of the proper financial support to also be deprived of a relationship with the parent who is supposed to be paying support. No matter how frustrated or angry you may be with the other parent, you must act maturely for the sake of your child. Remember that access and child support are the rights of the *child* that must be respected even if the other parent is not doing so. Do not discuss financial matters with the child or try to dissuade the child from seeing the other parent because of the default in payment. Let the government enforcement agency do its job to enforce the child support, and let your child enjoy his/her right to have a good relationship with the other parent. This point cannot be overemphasized.

Reducing or terminating child support to enforce access

If you are a noncustodial parent who is being denied access to your child, this is not your child's fault, so don't punish the child by cutting off your financial support. Whether or not you see your child, he/she still has to be housed, clothed, and fed. You must continue to pay child support unless a court orders otherwise. In fact, even if a court were to suspend or terminate your access, you would still have to pay child support unless the court were to order otherwise.

If you need to take action to enforce your access rights, there are legal steps you can take, depending on the law where you live (see Chapter 12). Consult a family law lawyer for advice tailored to your individual situation.

The extreme situations

As stated, the law in most jurisdictions will not allow a parent to enforce access rights by depriving the child of his/her right to financial support.[1] However, there have been some exceptional cases where a custodial parent's conduct was so extreme that a court found it necessary to terminate child support. For example, in one case the custodial parent kept the children in hiding for three years. In another case, the custodial parent moved with the child to a foreign country in violation of a court order. In both of these situations, the court suspended the child support until the child was returned to the jurisdiction so that access could resume.

There have also been cases in which a custodial parent's persistent actions to undermine and destroy the child's relationship with the other parent were found to be so reprehensible that child support was terminated. However, most courts will not terminate child support if doing so would be detrimental to the child. In other words, if the child's needs cannot adequately be met without the child support, it would be inappropriate to cut off the support because this would be punishing the child. No reasonable parent who loves his/her child should want that child to have a reduced lifestyle because of the other parent's wrongdoing. For this reason, it can be quite a challenge to convince a court to suspend or terminate child support by reason of a custodial parent's alienating behaviour.

Adult children

Depending on the law where you live, different considerations may apply when it comes to child support payable for adult children. Once a child has reached the age of majority, there is some expectation that he/she will have matured sufficiently to have an independent relationship with each parent. With adulthood comes the ability to think for oneself and to assess one's parents in their own right, without being influenced or pressured by others' views. Children of separated parents should grow up to understand that there are always two sides to every story. One hopes children will appreciate that, whatever their parents' opinions may be about each other, this should not affect how their parents feel about them or how they should feel about their parents.

It is not unreasonable to expect an adult child who wants to be financially supported throughout his/her post-secondary school education to be willing to have contact with the parent paying the support. An adult child who wants nothing to do with a parent may be faced with a parent who does not want to continue supporting him/her. Some courts have ruled that if the parent is blameless in the situation and did nothing to deserve being "cut off" by the child, the parent will not have to pay child support or may be allowed to pay a reduced amount.

As you can imagine, these cases are very unpleasant because they open up old wounds. Adult children who want nothing to do with a parent are usually eager to explain why they feel this way. Often their reasons go back many years and reveal much emotional pain. Parents whose children want financial support but nothing else from them are equally eager to describe how they have been wrongly accused of being bad parents. The court must evaluate all of the evidence and decide whether the parent bears any responsibility for the child's decision to terminate the parent-child relationship. If so, then the parent must continue to pay child support for so long as the child remains a dependant under the applicable family law.

I have seen cases in which a noncustodial parent made no effort whatsoever to see the child and then was surprised to find that the child (now an adult) wanted nothing to do with him/her. Sometimes the parent will argue that he/she was prevented by the other parent from seeing the child. However, if in all those years he/she never took any steps to try to get access to the child (for example, by bringing a court application), he/she may have difficulty convincing a court that he/she truly desired access.

I remember one case where a noncustodial parent did not want to see the child because he did not believe he was the child's father. When the child was eighteen years old, DNA paternity testing was done at the noncustodial parent's request, and it turned out he was the child's father. If only he had requested this test when the child was a baby and child support was first ordered, he could have had a wonderful relationship with his son all those years. He had paid support faithfully for eighteen years without wanting to see the child, and now the child (who was an adult) was a complete stranger to him and was not interested in starting a relationship. The child testified that he was offended and deeply hurt that he had been deprived of a father throughout his childhood, "all because my father didn't believe my mother when she told him that he was my father, and he waited so long to find out that she was right." In those circumstances, I found that the child was not unreasonable in the position he took, and I ordered the father to continue paying child support. I urged the child to reconsider his feelings, because in my opinion it is never too late to get to know your parents.

In another case, the parents had separated when their daughter was four years old. The child lived with her mother and had alternate weekend access with her father, who paid child support faithfully. The mother remarried when the child was seven years old, and the child developed a close bond with her mother's new husband. Eventually the daughter wanted less and less to do with her father, even though he had acted appropriately and done all he could to make access visits enjoyable for his daughter. By the time the child was a teenager, she was refusing to see her father except on rare special occasions and gave no reason why she was not interested in having a relationship with him. When the child turned nineteen, she legally changed her surname to that of her mother's husband and completely terminated her relationship with her father, who was heartbroken. She testified that although her father had done nothing wrong, her mother's husband was the one who had raised her and was therefore her "real" father. She said, "I have room in my heart for only one father figure, not two." Nevertheless, she thought that her biological father should continue paying child support to finance her university education because he had more money than her mother's husband. In that case, I ruled that the father was totally blameless for his daughter's decision to end her relationship with him. If she was going to consider her mother's husband to be her "real" father, then she should look to him for financial support. I terminated the father's child support obligations.

It bears repeating that the law is not the same in each jurisdiction, and it is essential to consult a family law lawyer for advice on whether your situation may entitle you to a reduction or termination of child support.

---

1   In some American jurisdictions, the court will suspend or terminate child support by reason of the custodial parent's violation of the support payor's visitation rights. Where this is permitted, the law imposes a high burden of proof on the payor to show that he/she made substantial and repeated efforts to see the child. Even if the payor succeeds in suspending or terminating child support, the court may choose not to eliminate any arrears that may have accrued. Consult a lawyer to find out whether these legal principles apply where you live.

CHAPTER TEN

PARALLEL CASES IN CRIMINAL AND FAMILY COURT

IT IS A SAD REALITY FOR A GREAT MANY SEPARATED COUPLES AND THEIR CHILDREN THAT THEY MUST CONTEND WITH NOT JUST ONE COURT CASE BUT TWO: one in family court and one in criminal court. There are even some families that have three court cases going on at the same time: a family case between the parents to deal with their custody, access, and financial issues (possibly including divorce); a criminal charge against one of the parents; and a court case brought against the parents by the child protection authorities. However, in this latter situation, the parents' court case dealing with custody and access is usually suspended until the child protection case is finished. This is because the child protection issues are of paramount concern and must be addressed before the parents can resume their private dispute. (For a discussion of the role of child protection authorities, see Chapter 11.)

Most of the time when separated parents find themselves in both criminal and family courts, the cases involve the same facts. That is why I have referred to the cases as being *parallel* cases. In the typical scenario, Parent A and Parent B will have had an argument or fight resulting in the police being called. One or both parents will be charged with having committed a criminal offence such as assault, threatening, criminal harassment, or perhaps an offence relating to property damage. Sometimes several criminal charges are laid, stemming from the same incident. For the purposes of this example, let us assume that Parent A is charged with assaulting Parent B. Very soon after the incident, Parent B comes to family court seeking a restraining order, custody of the children, and child support. This chapter will highlight the issues that can arise when parents are dealing with parallel criminal and family court cases.

Each court case has a different purpose
It is important to understand that the criminal case and the family case have different purposes, even though they relate to the same facts. The criminal justice system fulfills three basic objectives: (1) to punish people who misbehave and dissuade them from doing so in the future, (2) to deter others from misbehaving, and (3) to protect the public. In contrast, the family justice system is primarily intended to resolve parental disputes following family breakdown. There is a public component in the family justice system, in the sense that: (1) society has an interest in ensuring that the consequences of family breakdown are fair and in the best interests of the children affected, and (2) family courts hear child protection cases (dealing with child abuse or neglect) brought by child protection authorities. However, on the whole, family court deals with private matters, whereas the criminal court addresses the public interest in maintaining an orderly and safe society.

In a criminal court case, a person (called the *accused*) is charged with having committed a criminal offence. The parties in the case are the *prosecution* (in Canada and other Commonwealth countries, called the "Crown") and the *accused* (sometimes called the "defendant"). The prosecution must prove beyond a reasonable doubt that the offence was committed. The accused is presumed innocent until proven guilty, and has the right to remain silent — there is no obligation to present any defence evidence. If the prosecution is unable to prove beyond a reasonable doubt that the offence was committed, the accused must be found not guilty (called an *acquittal*).

It is important to understand that a finding of not guilty does *not* mean the person is innocent. Rather, it means the evidence did not establish with the necessary degree of certainty that the offence was committed. It may well be that the person actually committed the offence, but if the evidence presented in court does not convince the judge (or jury) beyond a reasonable doubt that the offence was committed, the accused must be acquitted.

In contrast to what happens in criminal court, there is no "prosecution" in family court; the only parties in the case are the parents.[1] In family court, there is no constitutional right to remain silent; the parties must present the necessary evidence to support their claims and respond to each other's claims. If one party fails to respond to the other's claim, it may be granted on a default basis (called an *uncontested order*). In addition, the standard of proof for decision making in family court is a *balance of probabilities, not proof beyond a reasonable doubt,* which is the standard applied in criminal court. (For more about the evidentiary standard of proof in family court, see Chapter 2.)

Inconsistent findings by criminal and family courts

What is the effect in family court of the result in a criminal court case? If a parent is convicted of a criminal offence, the family court will be bound by this ruling and will accept that the parent committed the act in question. In other words, it will not be open to that parent to argue in family court that he/she did not commit the offence. However, if the parent is acquitted in criminal court, or if for some reason the criminal charge is withdrawn, it is still possible for the family court to make a finding that the incident in question occurred. This is because the balance of probabilities standard of proof requires a lower degree of certainty than proof beyond a reasonable doubt. In other words, it is quite possible for a family court judge to conclude that Parent A *probably* assaulted Parent B, even though the evidence did not persuade the criminal court judge (or jury) *beyond a reasonable doubt* that Parent A assaulted Parent B.

What if the family court finds that Parent A assaulted Parent B? Does this ruling bind the criminal court and *require* that Parent A be convicted of the criminal offence of assault? The answer is no. Proof on a balance of probabilities can never be enough to justify a criminal finding of guilt. The criminal court will not find Parent A guilty unless the evidence satisfies the judge (or jury) that Parent A assaulted Parent B on the more rigorous standard of proof beyond a reasonable doubt. In other words, evidence that convinces a family court judge that Parent A *probably* assaulted Parent B may not be compelling enough to convince a judge or jury *beyond a reasonable doubt* that Parent A assaulted Parent B.

I mentioned earlier that a finding of guilt in criminal court will be binding on the family court, but this depends on the criminal court trial being held *before* the family court makes its decision. In practice, this almost never happens because decisions about whether to grant restraining orders and to settle the children's living arrangements must be made as soon as possible after separation. When parents are in dispute about these matters, the family court does not have the luxury of waiting for the criminal trial to be held. At the very least, the family court must make a temporary order to stabilize the family situation.

It is true that the temporary family court order could be changed or a trial could finally be held once the results of the criminal case are known, but as you know from Chapter 6, temporary orders can be difficult to change if this would disrupt the children's lives. You also know from Chapter 2 that trials are very rarely held, with the result that, in most cases, temporary orders end up determining the final outcome of the case. Obviously if a family court decision, even a temporary one, is being made before the criminal trial has been held, the family court judge will not know what the outcome of the criminal court case will be. There is a real possibility that the criminal and family court decisions will be inconsistent with each other.

There have been cases in which a family court was not satisfied on a balance of probabilities that Parent A assaulted Parent B, and yet a criminal court was satisfied beyond a reasonable doubt that the assault occurred. How could this happen if the standard of proof in family court is so much lower than in criminal court? If the evidence was not even compelling enough to convince a family court judge that Parent A *probably* assaulted Parent B, how could a criminal court judge (or jury) find *beyond a reasonable doubt* that the assault happened?

There can be several reasons for this apparent inconsistency. Different evidence may have been presented in each case. For example, medical records proving the injuries may have been presented in the criminal court case but not in the family court case. Witnesses who observed the incident may have testified in the criminal court case but not in the family court case. I have seen this happen in cases in which the assaulted party did not have a lawyer in the family court case and did not put the best available evidence before the court. In criminal court, this problem does not exist because the prosecution does all of the work in obtaining and presenting the evidence needed to prove the offence.

Sometimes the inconsistencies between findings made by criminal and family courts stem from the importance (or *weight*) applied to the witnesses' testimony. It is possible that a witness could be believed by one judge (or jury) but disbelieved by another. There is a human element to the justice system that cannot be ignored or avoided, particularly in the task of assessing the truthfulness (called *credibility*) of witnesses.

In assessing credibility, judges pay great attention to the cross-examination testimony of witnesses — that is, the answers witnesses give to questions posed by the other party (preferably by the other party's lawyer). A skilful cross-examination can highlight inaccuracies and inconsistencies in key details, helping the judge (or jury) decide whether a witness is being truthful. Without a thorough cross-examination, it can be difficult to assess the honesty and sincerity of a witness. In my experience, a major reason why a witness' testimony may be accepted in one case but rejected in another is because the testimony may not have been subjected to a proper cross-examination in one case but was in the other.

Get a lawyer!

Litigation lawyers spend years developing and perfecting their cross-examination skills in order to test the believability of witnesses' stories. Rarely have I encountered a litigant able to conduct an effective cross-examination on his/her own without legal counsel. This is one important reason why having a lawyer is highly advisable any time you are involved in a court proceeding, especially if there are important facts in dispute and the credibility of the parties or other witnesses will need to be assessed.

It can be upsetting and confusing for a parent who has been found not guilty in criminal court (or whose charge was withdrawn) to face the prospect in family court of being found to have committed the act in question. It can also be worrisome for a litigant whose conduct has already been judged in family court to have to contend with a parallel case in criminal court. It can be equally distressing for the party alleging that the act occurred. Imagine having to testify as a victim in criminal court and then having to essentially repeat this testimony in family court, only to face the prospect of inconsistent conclusions because of the different standards of proof in each court or because the evidence unfolded differently in each court.

Parents facing two court cases must decide how best to approach this situation. For example, should the same evidence be presented in each case? Does it matter which court case proceeds first? Should you try to get one case postponed until the other case is finished? Can the evidence used in one case be used for or against one of the parties in the other case? Can a statement by a party or finding of fact made in one case possibly affect the outcome in the other case? The answers to these questions can be complex and depend on the law where you live and the individual circumstances of each case. Only a lawyer with criminal law expertise can advise you on the appropriate strategy to take in dealing with your criminal charge. Only a family law lawyer can help you manage your family court case.

If you are charged with a criminal offence and also litigating in family court, is it possible to hire one lawyer to represent you in both cases? The answer is yes, but you should do this only if you can find a lawyer who has expertise in both criminal and family law. As you know from Chapter 5, many lawyers specialize in only one area of law, so it may be difficult to find a lawyer who has the knowledge and experience to represent you equally well in both cases. Most litigants I see who have parallel cases in criminal and family court hire a criminal lawyer to represent them in criminal court and a family law lawyer to represent them in family court. Of course, it is essential that the two lawyers be in contact with each other and coordinate their litigation strategies for their client's benefit. There is no question that it can be very costly to hire two lawyers, but litigation — particularly in two different courts at the same time — can be a nightmare to navigate without legal representation.

No-contact orders

When a person is charged with assaulting, threatening, or harassing a child or ex-partner, a decision must first be made whether to release the person on bail or keep him/her in jail until the trial. If the person is released on bail, there will almost certainly be conditions that he/she must obey until the criminal case is finished — that is, until the trial is over or the charge is withdrawn. Usually the bail order restricts the accused from having any contact or communication with or being anywhere near the person who is the alleged victim in the case. The bail order also usually prohibits the person from going to the alleged victim's home, place of employment, school, daycare provider, or any place where he/she might reasonably expect the alleged victim to be. These conditions are called *no-contact orders*.

If the accused person is found guilty in criminal court, he/she may be placed on probation for up to three years (possibly longer depending on the law where you live). The same no-contact conditions that were in the bail order might be included in the probation order. Depending on how long it takes for the criminal case to be finished and the probation order to expire, it is possible for a parent to be bound by no-contact conditions for a long time. This can have a serious impact on the parent's family court case and, more importantly, on the parent's relationship with his/her children.

Let us assume that Parent A is charged with assaulting Parent B. Parent A and Parent B have two young children. Immediately after the incident leading to the assault charge, Parent B comes to family court and obtains a temporary restraining order (see Chapter 3). The restraining order prohibits Parent A from having any contact or communication with Parent B or from coming within 500 metres of Parent B's home or place of employment. The order also provides that Parent A is to arrange access visits through a lawyer or another third party. The same day that the restraining order is made, Parent A is released on bail by the criminal court. The bail order contains a condition prohibiting Parent A from having any contact or communication whatsoever with Parent B, directly or indirectly. How is Parent A to arrange access visits through a third party (which is allowed under the restraining order) if the bail order prohibits any contact with Parent B, even indirect contact through a third party?

Unfortunately, it is a fairly frequent occurrence that conditions in criminal court bail orders are inconsistent with family court orders. Usually this is because the orders are made at different times, and neither court is made aware of the other court's order. Sometimes it is possible to have a bail order or restraining order changed to make the two orders consistent. Until the inconsistency is resolved, which order takes precedence? In most jurisdictions the criminal court bail order will take priority. This means that in the example above, Parent A may not be able to arrange access visits with his/her children until the bail order is changed or the criminal case is over.

I have seen many cases in which the parents wanted to move beyond the initial hostilities that occurred at the time of separation. They felt ready to begin the process of developing a peaceful and civilized working relationship as co-parents. However, they were unable to attend mediation[2] or counselling together because of a no-contact provision in a criminal court bail or probation order. In many cases, the custodial parent would be agreeable to having the other parent come to his/her home to pick up and return the children for access visits, but this is prohibited by a bail or probation order.

It can be frustrating for parents to contend with conflicting court orders. It can also be counterproductive and unhelpful to families if court-ordered restrictions no longer reflect their circumstances or needs. In recent years, there has been a growing effort by criminal and family court judges to be mindful of these considerations. Bail and probation orders can be worded to provide the flexibility needed to allow the family court to make orders that are practical for the parents and children while at the same time respecting safety concerns. For example, many criminal court no-contact conditions provide that "the accused shall have no contact or communication with [name of other parent] except to arrange access visits in accordance with a family court order." Following conviction, some probation orders state that the offender "shall have no contact with [name of other parent] except with that parent's express written consent which may be revoked at any time." Orders worded in this way provide for the possibility of some contact between the parents if the circumstances make it appropriate.

If you feel that you and your ex-partner and children could benefit from a change to the wording of a no-contact order, consult your lawyer right away. It is important to address this concern quickly, because the longer parent-child contact is being prevented, the more challenging it may be to get it resumed. Some noncustodial parents become virtual strangers to their children while they wait for no-contact orders to expire. This should not happen unless a court has determined that it is in the children's best interests to have no contact with the affected parent.

One final word of caution to persons who are bound by no-contact terms in bail, probation, or restraining orders. Remember that these are court orders, and there can be serious consequences for violating them. It can be tempting to ignore no-contact conditions if you and your ex-partner have "patched things up." I have seen many cases where the parent who was supposed to be protected by the no-contact order actually *initiated* contact with the person ordered to keep away! This is inappropriate and unfair to the parent who is bound by the no-contact order, and can put him/her in jeopardy of being charged with breaching the order. If you think that a no-contact order needs to be changed or terminated because the circumstances have changed since the order was made, you are urged to consult a lawyer to advise you on how best to address your situation.

Families are forever

It is a serious and frightening thing to be charged with a criminal offence. A conviction for an offence of violence against a spouse can carry grave consequences including incarceration. It is understandable that a parent in this situation might be preoccupied with the criminal court case and perhaps be inclined to pay less attention to the family court case. I routinely see parents hire lawyers in their criminal court cases but not in their family court cases. I find it interesting that when a parent only has enough money to pay for one lawyer, chances are he/she will spend that money to hire a criminal lawyer, not a family law lawyer. Parents seem to be much more willing to represent themselves in family court than in criminal court. This intrigues me.

Why do so many parents seem to invest more energy and resources in their criminal court cases than their family court cases? Isn't it obvious that long after the criminal case is over, the parent will have to deal with his/her family law issues of divorce, custody, access, support, and matrimonial property matters? When all is said and done, the criminal court case will be one episode (albeit extremely unpleasant) in a parent's life, but family relationships are forever. It is worth keeping in mind that eventually, most no-contact provisions in criminal court orders will expire, but no-contact provisions in family court restraining orders can last indefinitely.

I am not for a moment suggesting that criminal charges should not be taken seriously or that persons accused of criminal offences should not hire lawyers. Quite the contrary: criminal charges are very serious and accused persons should always have lawyers. What I am suggesting is that family court matters are at least equally important and should be taken just as seriously as criminal charges, because one's family relationships will continue long after a criminal case ends.

It is very important to be represented by a lawyer in both court cases. If you cannot afford a separate lawyer for each court case, then do your very best to find a lawyer who has the knowledge and experience to represent you in both cases. If this is not possible, and you only have money to hire one lawyer, you should at least consult with a criminal lawyer *and* a family lawyer. Get their advice about how best to allocate your available funds. You may be able to hire *both* lawyers to handle specific aspects of each case. For example, the criminal lawyer may conduct plea negotiations and/or represent you at your trial, and the family law lawyer may prepare all your family court documents and represent you at certain key court appearances such as motions. It cannot be overemphasized that you should make every effort to get as much assistance from a lawyer as possible in both court cases.

---

1   Custody and access cases can also involve other relatives. In addition, in child protection cases dealing with child abuse or neglect, the child protection agency will always be a party in the case.

2   As stated in Chapter 4, mediation may not be appropriate in cases in which domestic violence has occurred, particularly if one party is intimidated by or fearful of the other. This is not to say that mediation can never be available where domestic violence has occurred. In cases where the assault was of a minor nature and was an isolated incident in an otherwise non-violent relationship, mediation may be appropriate. A key factor is the ability of the victimized party to express his/her own needs. In some cases where domestic violence has occurred, "shuttle mediation" will occur; that is, the mediator meets with each party separately and "shuttles" between them. Each case depends on its own circumstances.

CHAPTER ELEVEN

WHEN PRIVATE DISPUTES BECOME A PUBLIC CONCERN:
CALLING IN THE CHILD PROTECTION AUTHORITIES

Child protection agencies

EVERY JURISDICTION HAS A GOVERNMENT-FUNDED CHILD PRO-
TECTION AGENCY WHOSE RESPONSIBILITY IS TO KEEP CHILDREN
SAFE FROM ABUSE OR NEGLECT. These agencies employ specially
trained social workers with broad legal powers to investigate and, if
necessary, apprehend (sometimes called *remove*) children whose physical or emotional safety is at risk, and to bring court cases against
their parents. The court has the power to place a child with relatives,
community members, or in foster care if the circumstances make it
necessary to protect the child. Every jurisdiction has a statute setting
out (1) the circumstances that must exist before a child protection

agency can intervene in a family's life or apprehend a child and (2) the legal test that must be met before a child can be temporarily or permanently taken away from his/her parents. For specific details about the law in your jurisdiction, consult a family law lawyer or your local child protection agency.

Child protection agencies can become involved in families in several ways. Sometimes one or both parents call the agency for assistance in arranging referrals to counselling, mediation, parenting courses, or other social services for themselves or their children. Sometimes a parent will call the agency to raise concerns about the care a child is receiving from the other parent. Such calls can also come from relatives, friends, neighbours, social service employees, teachers, doctors and other medical personnel, lawyers, clergymen, daycare workers, counsellors, and police officers. In most jurisdictions, professionals who work with children have a legal duty to report suspected child neglect or abuse to the child protection agency. This legal duty is so important it usually overrides any confidentiality rules that would normally apply to these professionals.[1]

I had one case where the police were conducting wiretap surveillance on a suspected drug trafficker. While listening to the telephone conversations coming from the suspect's home, the police could overhear a child being yelled at and beaten by an adult who resided in the home. The police contacted the child protection agency, which took immediate steps to investigate the care that the child was receiving. The child was apprehended and placed in foster care. This would have been the result in any event, because the parents ended up being arrested and incarcerated for drug trafficking, and there were no other family members available to care for the child.

There are cases in which the agency's contact with the family is prompted by an anonymous phone call or letter. Some family members, friends, and neighbours fear retaliation by the parents, so they contact the child protection agency anonymously. Sometimes agencies receive calls from total strangers who have observed parents mistreating their children in public places such as parking lots, stores, or parks. The agency is obliged to take seriously all information it receives and to investigate every allegation of child abuse or neglect.

A judge can also initiate the agency's involvement. During a court case, if a judge becomes concerned that a child may be suffering from abuse or neglect, or is at risk of being abused or neglected, the judge has the discretion to ask the child protection agency to investigate the situation. I once had a case involving a three-year-old child, whose prostitute mother slept with her clients and the child in the same bed. The father was a convicted child molester. After hearing all the evidence, I was not satisfied that either parent was a suitable caregiver. I arranged for the child protection agency to intervene, and the child was temporarily placed in foster care. Luckily, a responsible family member came forward and was granted custody of the child.

Intervention by child protection agency in custody disputes

The previous case is an extreme but obvious example of a situation in which the involvement of child protection authorities was necessary. However, the circumstances do not necessarily have to be extreme for parents to find themselves facing intervention by child protection authorities. Many parents embroiled in high-conflict custody and access disputes do not realize that their conduct may be placing their children at risk of suffering *emotional harm*. Although each jurisdiction has its own legal definition of *abuse* and *neglect,* virtually every child protection statute includes emotional harm as a basis for intervention by a child protection agency. It is universally agreed by child welfare professionals that children who are caught in the middle of high-conflict custody disputes can be at risk of suffering emotional harm, which is most definitely a form of child abuse.

A child caught in the middle of a toxic tug of war between parents can suffer emotional harm in numerous ways:

1) The child might be witnessing vicious parental arguments, which can be extremely frightening. It can undermine a child's sense of security and well-being and can make him/her afraid for his/her future.

2) One or both parents (or, for that matter, other relatives) may be making inappropriate comments to the child about the parental dispute, or demeaning the other parent and urging the child to take sides. This is damaging to a child because it is very confusing and unsettling for a child to have an important figure in his/her life demeaned. Parents are role models for children; children learn how to treat people by their par-

ents' examples. Many children in parental tugs of war end up having academic difficulties and troubles in their personal relationships. Some children have anger problems leading to involvement with the criminal justice system.

3) The custodial parent may be interfering with the child's right of access to the other parent. The child might even be abducted or taken into hiding by a parent in order to cut the other parent out of the child's life. I once had a case in which the custodial parent refused to send the child to school in order to keep the other parent from knowing where the child was. There have been cases in which the custodial parent fabricated false accusations of child sexual abuse against the other parent, subjecting the child to numerous unnecessary medical examinations and interviews by doctors, social workers, and police — all in a desperate effort to keep the other parent away from the child.

There is no end to the tactics some parents will resort to in their quest for power, control, and vengeance. Parents need to understand that such behaviour can cause devastating and long-lasting emotional damage to their children. Moreover, parents who conduct themselves with such complete lack of concern for their children may be sending a clear message to the court that they are not suitable to have custody. In fact, they may end up not only losing custody but being granted only supervised access to their children.

Working voluntarily with a child protection agency

In cases in which parental disputes are putting children at risk of suffering harm, child protection agencies have a duty to get involved. Usually the agency's first approach will be to ask parents to co-operate voluntarily by participating in counselling, assessments, and other programs to address the child protection concerns. The agency's social workers can be of great assistance to families if the parents are willing to take the steps recommended to them. If you are ever contacted by a child protection agency because of concerns regarding your child, you should see this as an offer of assistance rather than an attack. Take advantage of the opportunity to meet with the agency's social workers and avail yourself of the resources being offered to help you, your ex-partner, and your children. You are certainly welcome to consult a lawyer as well, to help you understand this process and make sure that any expectations of the agency are clear. If the society is raising allegations that might involve criminal charges, then you should definitely consult a lawyer.

Ideally, both parents should work co-operatively with the agency. Sadly, this does not always happen. When only one parent, not both, is causing emotional harm to a child, that parent may be too lacking in maturity and insight to appreciate the agency's role, which is to protect children. In such cases, the other parent may find the agency to be of great help. For example, the agency may support his/her custody claim in family court, by providing a letter explaining its concerns for the child's welfare arising from the other parent's behaviour. The agency might also be willing to act as an intermediary between the parents to arrange access visits and possibly even supervise the noncustodial parent's access. Most importantly, the agency can help get the child engaged in counselling and therapy to address the emotional damage caused by the other parent's conduct.

Court cases brought by child protection agency

If the agency believes it is not getting the necessary co-operation from the parents on a voluntary basis, it can commence a court action against the parents. In an urgent case, the agency can apprehend a child and place him/her in foster care even before seeing a judge. Once the court action starts, the parents will find themselves not only litigating against each other but, more importantly, against the child protection agency. In my opinion, this is the "ground zero" for any custody dispute: a private matter stemming from a parental separation has now become the subject of government intervention to protect a child from abuse or neglect.

In most child protection cases triggered by custody and access conflicts, the agency asks the court to make a finding that the child was, at the time the case started, suffering from emotional harm or at risk of such harm.[2] The court will review the evidence presented by the agency and the parents. The judge's first task will be to decide where the child will be temporarily placed until the trial. The child may be placed with a parent, relative, family friend, community member, or, as a last resort, foster care. In making a temporary order, the court will select the least intrusive option that will eliminate the risk of harm to the child. This means that consideration should always be given to placing a child with family before placing a child with strangers in a foster home. Once the temporary placement is chosen, the court will also have to decide the appropriate access. For example, if the child is placed with a parent, the visitation schedule for the other parent will have to be determined; if the child is placed with a grandparent or in foster care, the visitation schedule for both parents will need to be arranged.

If the court places the child with a parent or family member, conditions can be imposed to address the risks that caused the agency to start the court case. For example, access by certain persons may have to be supervised either by an agency social worker or a responsible adult selected by the court. In cases triggered by parental tugs of war, the court might impose a condition preventing a child from being in the presence of both parents at the same time, to protect the child from witnessing parental arguments. Other conditions may require one or both parents to participate in counselling or parenting education programs. The child protection agency will supervise the child's placement to ensure that the child is being well cared for and that the court-ordered conditions are being obeyed. If the conditions are breached, the agency can take appropriate action, including apprehending the child, if necessary.

If the parents and the agency are not able to settle the case by agreement, there will be a trial. Like custody cases, there can be a long delay before a trial date is reached. Court backlogs, lawyers' schedules, waiting periods for assessments, therapy, and counselling can all contribute to delays. Some children spend a long time in temporary foster care waiting for a trial to occur so a final decision can be made about their futures. There is no question that once a child protection agency starts a court case, parents must be prepared to have the agency involved in their lives for a very long time.

At the trial, if the judge finds that the child was indeed suffering from emotional harm (or at risk of suffering from such harm) when the case started, a child protection order will be made. The judge will then have to decide on a placement for the child that will be in the child's best interests (called a *disposition order*). All of the placements considered at the temporary stage can again be considered, plus any new plans for the child that may have been developed since then. If the child is placed with a parent, relative, or community member, the agency will supervise the placement to ensure the child is being well cared for and that he/she is not being exposed to the problems that necessitated the agency's intervention in the first place.

Depending on the applicable law, the court can make a series of placement orders stretching several years if necessary. For example, at the end of the trial, the court may place the child with a grandparent for six months under the agency's supervision, with appropriate conditions that must be complied with, and access to each parent on alternating weekends. When the six months have expired, the agency will return the case to court for a review of the situation (called a *status review* or, in some jurisdictions, *permanency hearings*). At the status review hearing, the judge will decide whether any child protection concerns still exist and if so, what placement would be in the child's best interests. In our example, if the parents have not made sufficient progress to develop a workable parenting plan that protects the child from their conflict, the court might extend the child's placement with the grandparent (again under agency supervision, with appropriate conditions) for another six months. This situation could go on for years with one placement order being made after another. The court case will remain alive as long as the child protection concerns remain unaddressed.

If a child has been placed in foster care, there are strict timelines dictating how long a child can remain in this situation of "legal limbo." It is unfair to keep children waiting indefinitely in the hopes that their parents may someday solve the child protection problems. In the jurisdiction where I preside, a child under the age of six years can be kept in temporary foster care only twelve months. Children six years of age or older can be kept in temporary foster care for a maximum of twenty-four months. Once these limitation periods have expired, the child must either be placed with a parent, relative, or community member; if this is not possible, the parental rights must be terminated. When parental rights are terminated, the child is no longer the *legal* child of the parents; the child becomes the legal child of the government. Once this happens, it may be possible for the child to be placed for adoption, or the child may remain in foster care and continue to have visitation with parents and other family members. The law regarding termination of parental rights and adoption is different in each jurisdiction. For information about the child protection laws where you live, consult a family law lawyer or your local child protection agency.

As you might expect, child protection cases can be very stressful. The parents must prepare written materials responding to the agency's allegations. They must each provide a proposal (called a *plan of care*) detailing how they plan to address the child protection concerns and meet the child's best interests in the future. They must attend frequent meetings with the agency's social workers, who will assess each parent's plan and conduct home studies on all potential caregivers for the child. There will be numerous court appearances at which the judge will be assisting the parties to explore solutions. These steps must be taken not only in the initial child protection application brought by the agency but also in every status review application until the case is finally finished.

If you are involved in a court case with a child protection agency, you are well advised to hire a family law lawyer who has knowledge and experience in child protection cases. If you and your ex-partner are in disagreement over the facts of the case or the most desirable placement for the child, you will need to hire separate lawyers. The same lawyer cannot represent two people whose positions are in conflict with each other (see Chapter 5). In fact, in a child protection case triggered by parental conflict, I cannot imagine the same lawyer *ever* being able to represent both parents. The importance of having legal representation in child protection cases cannot be overemphasized. This area of the law is complex and there are many procedural rules that must be followed. Without a lawyer's help, you may have great difficulty navigating your way through the child protection litigation.

You may be wondering what happens to the custody and access litigation between the parents when a child protection agency decides to start its own court case against the parents. In most jurisdictions, the law provides that the parents' custody dispute must take a back seat to the child protection case. This means that the parents' custody case will be suspended and simply lie dormant until the child protection case is finished. Depending on the circumstances of the case, this could take years. As I stated above, once a child protection agency gets involved, it will remain involved until a long-term plan for the child is established. The court case will not end until the judge is satisfied that the parental behaviour creating the risk to the children is not likely to recur.

My purpose in writing this chapter is to sound an alarm bell. Very few disputing parents ever put their minds to the possibility that a child protection agency might start a court case against them. Even fewer parents contemplate the risk of losing their children due to emotional harm caused by being in the middle of parental tugs of war. Think of the trauma that you and your children might endure if a child protection agency found it necessary to apprehend your children and place them with a relative or in foster care. You can take positive steps to make sure this never happens. Get the counselling, therapy, parenting education, and legal advice you need to (1) understand your own role in perpetrating the conflict, (2) learn how to shield your children from the conflict, and (3) learn how to resolve the conflict. Remember, it's all about maturity!

If you think that your custody dispute is getting out of hand to the extent that your ex-partner's actions may be putting your child's emotional well-being at risk, contact your local child protection agency for assistance. You may wish to consult your lawyer before calling the child protection agency, because it is a serious thing to report your ex-partner to the child protection authorities. You want to be certain that the conduct you are complaining about is serious enough to justify their intervention. You also do not want your act of calling the child protection agency to be perceived as a form of personal attack on your ex-partner or a litigation strategy tactic. This being said, the welfare of your child must always be your paramount concern. If you believe that your child is at risk of harm for any reason, your local child protection agency is there to help you.

---

1   As a general rule, all communications between a lawyer and his/her client are confidential and cannot be disclosed by the lawyer to anyone without the client's consent. The question of whether a lawyer is required to report suspected child abuse or neglect if doing so would violate lawyer-client confidentiality depends on the laws of the applicable jurisdiction.

2   There are numerous grounds that could justify a child protection order, such as infliction of physical harm or risk of such harm, sexual abuse, abandonment, failure to provide necessary medical treatment, and other grounds. However, in most cases stemming from parental conflict over custody and access, the ground relied upon by child protection agencies is emotional harm or risk of emotional harm.

CHAPTER TWELVE

SO NOW WHAT? AFTER YOUR DISPUTE IS RESOLVED

THERE ARE GENERALLY TWO WAYS A DISPUTE CAN BE RESOLVED: THE PARTIES CAN REACH AN AGREEMENT OR SOMEONE ELSE CAN MAKE THE DECISION. Family law disputes are no different. However, one unique aspect of family law agreements and decisions is that they last a very long time — usually until the children grow up and finish school, although they can last much longer if spousal support (sometimes called *alimony*) is involved. During the life of a family law agreement or decision, new issues and disputes can arise. There can be difficulties relating to enforcement of terms relating to property, support, custody, or access. One or both parties may want to terminate or change some aspect of the decision or agreement. This chapter will explain the ways in which the justice system can deal with family law agreements and decisions after they have been made.

Contracts

The most common way for ex-partners to settle their affairs is by way of contract. Some couples enter into contracts, called *marriage contracts* or *cohabitation agreements,* early in the relationship. These contracts determine how the couple's property and financial affairs will be dealt with in the event of a separation. Matters relating to the custody, access, and support of children should not be included in marriage contracts or cohabitation agreements. It is impossible to predict, months or years before a separation, what the family's circumstances will be in the future if and when the parties separate. Custody and access decisions must be based on a child's best interests, having regard to the family's *current* circumstances, not the situation that existed when the contract was made (which may even be before the child was born). The same is true for child support: the amount depends on the payor's *current* income, not his/her income when the contract was made. In any event, the court is never bound by agreements regarding custody and access; the best interests of the child must prevail, and the court will ignore any parenting arrangement that does not meet this test.

Although there is no way to know for sure, I would guess that relatively few couples enter into marriage contracts or cohabitation agreements because most couples hope their relationships will last forever and do not even want to think about the prospect of breaking up. For couples that did not pre-arrange the financial consequences of a possible breakup, the task of settling these matters must be done at the time of separation or at some point afterwards. Most couples do this by entering into a contract called a *separation agreement*. A separation agreement will typically deal with all matters arising from the separation: a parenting plan for the children, child support, spousal support, division of property, payment of debts, and any other matters needing to be resolved on a final basis. Most jurisdictions provide a mechanism for separation agreements to be filed with the court so they can be enforced and possibly varied as if they were court orders.

Even if the parties are not able to reach an agreement and a court case is started, it is still very common for a settlement to be reached during the life of the court case. As I have stated, very few cases proceed all the way to trial, and once a temporary order has been made regarding custody, access, and support, the vast majority of family court litigants reach a final agreement. Sometimes the terms of the agreement are negotiated between the parties themselves (preferably with legal advice), or their lawyers, or perhaps a mediator was involved. The agreement becomes a contract called a *consent* or *minutes of settlement*, which can be filed with the court and made into a court order. The parties can even decide to enter into a separation agreement and withdraw the court case if they do not feel a court order is necessary. Many couples go to court just to get a divorce order and then address all of their other issues by way of separation agreement.

You should never enter into a marriage contract, cohabitation agreement, or separation agreement without first getting thorough legal advice from a family law lawyer. Each party must have a separate lawyer who is in no way connected to the other party or his/her lawyer. This is called obtaining *independent legal advice.* Only a lawyer can advise you on your legal rights and on the all-important question of whether you have all of the necessary information — especially about the other party's financial circumstances — to make an informed decision. This cannot be overemphasized. If you want to maximize the chances of your agreement being truly final, binding, and upheld by a court of law, it is absolutely essential that you and your ex-partner be properly represented by legal counsel.

There have been cases in which one party to an agreement later feels that the contract (or certain parts of it) should not be binding because of the circumstances that existed when it was entered into. In most jurisdictions, a family law agreement can be nullified (sometimes called *rescinded* or *set aside*) if one party behaved unfairly toward the other party while the contract was being negotiated. If one party pressured, threatened or took unfair advantage of the other party, a court might rule that the contract (or certain parts of it) should be ignored or changed because of *undue influence* or *duress.* For example, if Parent A tells Parent B that Parent B will never see the children again unless Parent A gets to keep all of the matrimonial property, this would be an example of an inappropriate attempt to pressure Parent B. Similarly, if during the contract negotiations one party failed to provide the other with *all* the details of his/her financial situation (called *financial disclosure*), a court may end up setting aside and changing the financial terms of the contract. This is because the law expects ex-partners to treat each other fairly, which requires each party to *completely reveal his/her entire financial circumstances* to the other.

Even if there has not been duress, undue influence, or a failure to provide full financial disclosure, a contract can still be set aside or changed if it is *unconscionable* — that is, if its terms are so overwhelmingly unfair as to shock the conscience of any reasonable person. For example, assume that Parent A and Parent B were married for twenty-five years. Parent A owns a successful business and is a millionaire. Parent B worked in Parent A's business for many years and contributed greatly to its success. Parent B was also the primary caregiver of the three children of the marriage and gave up the chance to pursue a lucrative career in favour of raising a family and helping to build up Parent A's business. At the time of separation, Parent A fired Parent B, who is now unemployed and clinically depressed. Soon after the separation, Parent A and Parent B entered into a separation agreement providing that Parent A will pay Parent B a very low monthly sum of spousal support for a period of two years, after which Parent B is expected to be self-supporting. Parent B is to receive no other property or payments. Parent B says that he/she entered into the agreement at a time of great emotional distress and he/she "just wanted to get it over with." In these circumstances, a court might well find the agreement to be unconscionable, and set it aside, and then make an appropriate property and support order in keeping with each party's rights and obligations under the law.

Sometimes a party to a contract wants to have it changed (called *varied* or *modified*) not so much because of the circumstances at the time it was entered into but because of the circumstances existing at the present time. This might be because at the time the contract was entered into, the parties anticipated that some event would happen — and then it didn't. Or the request to change the contract might be triggered by an event that neither party could have reasonably foreseen. This most often happens in contracts dealing with spousal support, because most ex-spouses try to reach final agreements that cannot be changed so they can get on with their lives and organize their future finances with certainty. Unfortunately, life is unpredictable, and the law can in certain circumstances allow an ex-spouse to reopen the issue of spousal support, even if the contract was intended to be final and unchangeable.

For example, assume that Parent A agreed to pay Parent B spousal support for two years, as it was expected that Parent B would go back to school for one year to upgrade his/her skills and then get a well-paying job. If after the contract was signed, Parent B became ill, was not able to obtain the necessary diploma, or could not find a job in his/her field, the spousal support may need to be changed so that Parent B is treated fairly. Or maybe Parent A has fallen ill and taken early retirement. Or maybe one of the parties has won the lottery! There are all kinds of unanticipated events that can occur after a contract is entered into that turn the future into something other than what everyone thought it would be. If certain legal tests are met (depending on the law where you live), it might be possible to have parts (or all) of a contract set aside or changed, particularly as they relate to spousal support.

I mentioned earlier that the court is never bound by agreements regarding custody and access. Nor can these agreements ever be truly "final" in the sense of being unchangeable. This is because a court must ensure that children's parenting arrangements meet their best interests on an ongoing basis. If a significant change of circumstances occurs at some point after an agreement is entered into, either parent (or both) may apply to the court to change the custody or access. For example, a parent might develop a substance abuse problem, or remarry, or move away, or change work hours — any of these changes might affect a child's best interests, depending on the circumstances. Or a child might develop special needs that require a different parenting arrangement than originally planned. No matter what parents may have originally agreed to, the court (if asked by either parent) will review all of the circumstances and make whatever custody and access order is in the best interests of the child.

Another matter that is never binding on the court is child support. Although parents are free to make whatever agreements they want for the financial support of their children, this is actually true only so long as the parents agree to live with their agreements. If at any time a parent applies to the court to have child support assessed according to the applicable law, the court will not hesitate to do so if the child support terms of the parents' agreement were unfair to the child.

For example, some parents enter into agreements stating that instead of paying child support, the noncustodial parent will give the custodial parent more than his/her fair share of the matrimonial property. If it later turns out that the overly generous property settlement does not meet the child's current needs, a court might order additional child support. The court has an overriding responsibility to make sure that children receive proper support. Child support is the right of the *child,* and the parents cannot bargain away this right. In any event, child support should be reviewed annually to ensure that the correct amount is being paid in accordance with the payor's income.

Until a court finds that a contract is no longer binding, or makes an order changing it, the parties are required to obey its terms. The law defining the grounds to have all or part of a contract set aside or varied differs from one jurisdiction to the next, and is complex. If you have questions about the legality or enforceability of any contract you have entered into, or if you want to change its terms, consult a lawyer. Do not simply take the law into your own hands by violating the contract, as there can be serious consequences for doing this. Get legal advice, as it will likely be necessary to start a court case if your ex-partner is insisting that the contract continue in effect.

Arbitration orders

As stated in Chapter 4, it is possible in most jurisdictions to have a family law decision made by an arbitrator selected by the parties. If the law where you live allows this, it will also provide a mechanism for making arbitration decisions enforceable. The most common way to do this is to file the arbitration decision with the court, which gives it the effect of a court order for enforcement purposes. The question of how to go about appealing or changing an arbitration decision depends on the law, the terms of the arbitration agreement, and the arbitrator's decision. You should consult a family lawyer to assist you.

Court orders

Appeals

If the court decided your family law issues, a court order would set out the terms with which both parties must comply. If one party is unhappy with the court order, it is possible to appeal to a higher court. However, an appeal will succeed only if the party filing the appeal (called the *appellant*) can show that the lower court judge misunderstood the evidence, failed to apply the law correctly, or committed some other serious error. The fact that you disagree with the judge's decision is not enough to justify an appeal.

Appeals in family law are rare for several reasons. First, they are expensive. A complete transcript of the hearing in the lower court must be ordered and paid for by the appellant. Legal fees must be paid to the lawyer conducting the appeal on your behalf. Secondly, appeals take a long time to be heard, as it can take a long time for the lower court transcript to be prepared, and appeal courts are very busy hearing appeals from many different kinds of cases.

Moreover, the mere fact of launching an appeal does not usually suspend the order being appealed from. In other words, unless the appellant can convince the appeal court to suspend (or *stay*) the order being appealed, that order will continue in effect until the appeal is heard. For example, if the court grants custody to Parent A and then Parent B files an appeal, Parent A will continue to have custody of the child unless the appeal court makes a temporary order imposing a different custody arrangement until the appeal is heard. Since appeals take such a long time to be heard, this creates an even longer status quo (see Chapter 6), which an appeal court may be reluctant to disrupt even if it finds that the trial judge did make an error.

Appeals are complex legal cases that absolutely require the assistance of legal counsel. You should not attempt to file an appeal on your own, as this can be a costly and frustrating experience. You need to obtain legal advice about the likelihood of success. Keep in mind that if your appeal is unsuccessful, you will very likely be ordered to pay all or part of the other party's costs in addition to your own.

Changing court orders

If an important change in circumstances occurs after an order has been made, it may be possible to have the order changed. As a general rule, orders dealing with matrimonial property cannot be changed. These are one-time orders that require property transfers or lump sums to be paid, and once this has been done, there is nothing to change because the transaction is finished. As always, if you have questions about any aspect of your family court order, consult a family law lawyer.

The four matters that are most commonly the subject of change requests (sometimes called applications or motions for *variation* or *modification*) are custody, access, spousal support, and child support.

Custody and access

As you know from Chapter 6, custody and access decisions are governed by the best interests of the child. If an important (sometimes called *material*) change in circumstances occurs after the court makes a custody or access order, either parent may start a fresh court case to ask for a change in the order. The judge's first task will be to decide whether the circumstances have changed enough since the court order was made to justify a fresh look at the parenting arrangements. If so, the court will review the entire situation and decide what changes to the court order must be made to meet the child's best interests. (The same factors explained in Chapter 6 will apply.)

As you might expect, it is relatively rare that custody gets changed because children need stability and should only have to change homes for a very good reason. However, access arrangements can change frequently throughout a childhood because children's needs change as they grow older. For example, if a parent had little involvement with a six-month-old baby prior to the separation, access might start with two-hour visits several times a week. After the parent has shown for a period of time that he/she can manage the child and exercise access in a responsible fashion, access can progress to full-day visits. As the child and parent adjust to the longer visits, access might progress to overnight visits. There is no fixed schedule for gradually increasing access as children grow; each case depends on its individual circumstances.

As children enter school, and then become involved in extracurricular activities, access schedules may have to change. Similarly, schedules may have to be adjusted to accommodate parents' work schedules and the travel time between their homes if one or both parents move. Much time is spent in family court assisting parents to reach mutually agreeable access schedules. In my opinion, the key to success is to be reasonable and flexible with the other parent. Both parents must appreciate that the child needs consistency, stability, and peace in order to learn well at school and be emotionally healthy. If each access visit begins and ends in a stressful way for the child (for example, by witnessing parental arguments over lateness, cancellations, conflicting holiday plans, and so on), this can be very harmful to the child's well-being.

A great number of access change motions that I see could be prevented if parents followed these tips:

1) Don't be late. If your order requires you to be at a certain location at the beginning or end of access visits, be there on time. When you are consistently late, you are sending a message to the other parent that only you matter, and that you

have no respect for him/her. It is not fair to keep people waiting for you. Anyone can be late once or twice due to traffic or weather conditions, but it is unacceptable when this happens consistently.

2) Don't cancel visits. Your children should be able to count on you. Don't disappoint them. If the access schedule is not practical for you to follow, speak to the other parent about possibly changing it. If you cannot reach an agreement to change the schedule, consult a lawyer to start a court case to change the access order. Too many parents do neither; they just cancel one visit after another, disappointing their children and aggravating the other parent. By the way, this rule applies to both the custodial and the noncustodial parent. Neither parent should cancel visits without a very good reason. It should also go without saying that any time a custodial parent cancels an access visit, arrangements should be made for a compensating makeup visit.

3) If you know that certain people upset the other parent, keep them away from each other. I never cease to be amazed at how many parents continually expose each other to their relatives and new partners when they know full well that there is friction between them. Don't make your ex-partner have to speak to these people on the phone, and don't bring them with you to access exchanges. Parents should deal with each other whenever possible. If this is not possible because of a restraining order or because the parents cannot behave civilly in front of their child, then choose a neutral person to arrange pickups and dropoffs. Be smart and do your part to keep the peace. Your goal should be to make access a pleasant experience for everyone, especially the child.

4) Be proactive and plan ahead for holiday time. Many court orders do not specify exact dates when the noncustodial parent is to have the child during vacation periods. For example, an order might provide a parent with "access for one week during the Christmas holiday period, two weeks in July and two weeks in August." Orders worded in this way contemplate that the parents will be able to agree on the access schedule *well in advance* of the holiday period each

155

year. But if you go to any family court during the months of December, June, July, and August, you will likely see dozens of parents in heated disputes over how to share their children's vacation time. Every December (especially the week before Christmas), I am confronted with cases in which each parent has paid for air travel and hotel in opposite ends of the world for exactly the same dates! And their tickets are always non-refundable! I am then expected to decide which parent gets to take the child during the period in question. Why didn't these parents solidify their access schedules well in advance? Everyone knows when the Christmas holiday period will be, and yet so many parents fail to communicate effectively with each other, leading to wasted money, tremendous anger and bitterness, disappointed children, and very distressed judges! This can all be so easily avoided if parents settle their vacation access schedules well in advance. If by the end of September (at the latest) you and your ex-partner have not agreed *in writing* to a Christmas access schedule, come to court before you pay for any trips. Similarly, if by the end of April (at the latest) you and your ex-partner have not agreed *in writing* to a summer access schedule, come to court. Vacation access schedules should never become emergencies.

If these four simple common-sense rules were followed, I have no doubt that a large number of court cases dealing with access change requests would be unnecessary. Be reasonable and fair with your ex-partner over access issues. This is a key aspect of maturity, which is the hallmark of a responsible parent.

Spousal support

As mentioned, the law regarding spousal support is different in each jurisdiction. For example, in Canada, unmarried partners (sometimes called *common law* couples) and same-sex couples can have spousal support obligations. However, in most American states, there are no spousal support rights for unmarried couples or same-sex couples. In addition, in those places where spousal support is possible, the legal rules regarding entitlement, duration, and amount can differ. The law can also differ from place to place on the question of whether a spousal support order can be changed if a change in circumstances occurs after a court order has been made. If you have a spousal support order and are wondering whether it might be possible to change or terminate it, you are well advised to consult a family law lawyer. Your lawyer will review your situation and advise you on how the law would likely apply to it.

Child support

Most jurisdictions provide that a noncustodial parent must pay child support in an amount properly reflecting his/her annual income. As most people's incomes change every year, it is necessary to ensure that the amount of child support is keeping up with the changes in the parents' incomes and the special expenses of the children (for example, daycare). For this reason, it is common for the amount to be adjusted many times over the course of a childhood.

Since the amount of child support is generally based on the payor's income, the law in most jurisdictions expects support payors to provide recipients with ongoing proof of income. This proof usually takes the form of the payor's income tax return and notice of assessment every year. In addition, if the parents are sharing additional expenses for such things as daycare, medical and dental fees, summer camp, and extracurricular activities, each parent will have to provide the other with proof of annual income. The support recipient will also have to provide the payor with proof (invoices, receipts, cancelled cheques, and so on) of the additional expenses.

In most cases, parents are able to agree on the amount of child support each year once they have exchanged the necessary financial disclosure. If full disclosure is not being provided, or if the parents cannot agree on the amount of a parent's annual income or on the appropriateness of an additional expense, a court case may be necessary.

Support payors should be aware that they have an obligation to be fair. Parents should support their children because they love them and because it's the right thing to do, not because of the law or a court order. It's part of being a good parent. Children have a right to be financially supported in accordance with their parents' ability to pay. If after a support order is made, a payor's income substantially increases, he/she has an obligation to let the recipient know and to increase the child support accordingly. If this is not done, the court may order a retroactive increase in the amount of child support dating back to the date of the payor's increased income. The law governing retroactive child support is not the same everywhere, so it is important to consult a lawyer if you have questions about the proper effective date of a support increase.

Of course, the amount of child support can go down as well as up. If a support payor's financial circumstances have changed for the worse since the order was made, it is important to act promptly to have the support amount adjusted accordingly. Don't just stop paying and hope the problem will go away — it won't. Not only will you accumulate arrears, but there is likely to be enforcement action taken against you by a government agency, and this will not be pleasant. The sooner this issue is dealt with, the better, as it will usually be necessary to retroactively change the amount of support from the date that the payor's income went down. As you might expect, it is never welcome news to a custodial parent that a request is being made to lower child support. Support payors in this situation will need to provide complete proof of the reason for the decreased income. For example, if you have been laid off or discharged from work, provide documentary proof from your employer. If you have suffered an illness or injury causing your income to go down, provide a report from your doctor explaining the nature of your disability, its expected duration, and its impact on your ability to work. If you have decided to change careers, be prepared to explain why this career change is reasonable given your child support obligations.

Many support payors seek a reduction in child support because they have entered new relationships and have new children to support. The question of whether and to what extent the existence of new children can affect a payor's pre-existing child support obligation is legally and morally complex. Some people feel that a parent should not be able to reduce his/her obligation to a child by having more children — after all, the child was there first and the payor should be assumed to have the ability to support the new children if he/she chose to have them. Others feel that this approach punishes the new children who, after all, are innocent in this discussion, and who deserve just as much to be properly supported as the payor's first child. If a payor cannot afford to pay the proper amount of child support to the first child *and* adequately support his/her new children, this creates a dilemma with no easy solutions. No court order can make someone rich! Most child support laws provide some possibility for an adjustment because of a payor's new family obligations, but this very much depends on the circumstances of the case. As a general rule it is fair to say that a payor in this situation may have an uphill battle. The moral of the story is: if you are going to have children, plan on supporting all of them.

Support of adult children

In most jurisdictions, parents are required to support their children until they finish school. If a child attends university, this can mean that child support will be payable until the child graduates, which could be around the age of twenty-three or twenty-four years, or maybe older. Most child support laws treat adult children differently than minor children. Although parents have an obligation to support their adult children until they graduate from school, some children are expected to contribute to their own education costs. The court must consider all of the circumstances, including the parents' incomes, the availability of funds from education savings plans, the child's income from part-time work and summer jobs, the cost and duration of the child's course of education, the availability of student loans and grants, and the reasonableness of a child's choice to attend an out-of-town school instead of living with a parent to save expenses. You will recall from Chapter 9 that in certain situations the court may even consider the nature of the relationship between the adult child and the parent being asked to pay child support.

As a general rule, the court has a lot of discretion to apportion the child's post-secondary education costs between the parents and, if appropriate, the child. In some cases, one parent is required to pay all of the child's expenses. In other cases, the support payor is required to pay the table amount (see Chapter 8) to the other parent plus only a modest contribution toward the child's tuition and books. Sometimes, the child support is paid to the child directly instead of to the custodial parent. If you, your ex-partner and adult child are unable to agree on the amount of child support, consult a family law lawyer. Your lawyer will advise you of how the law in your area deals with the support of adult children. Similarly, if you are a support payor who is unsure whether your adult child remains entitled to child support, speak to a lawyer.

Although some jurisdictions have cutoff ages (such as eighteen or twenty-one) when child support terminates, most jurisdictions require parents to support their children until they graduate from school. It is crucial that the support recipient notify the payor (and especially the support enforcement agency if applicable) as soon as the child has finished school, so that the payor will know to stop making payments. If the recipient fails to do this, the law may require him/her to reimburse the payor for any overpayments.

The involvement of social assistance authorities

One final word to parents wishing to change the amount of support. If at any time since the order or agreement was made, the support recipient has received welfare benefits (sometimes called "social assistance"), it will likely be necessary to involve the welfare authorities. This is because a person who receives welfare is almost always required to transfer or *assign* his/her support rights to the government, so that the public purse can be reimbursed for welfare funds paid out. This means that the support funds payable during the period the recipient received welfare are actually owed to the government. Consequently, a payor wishing to reduce or eliminate his/her support obligations during that period must deal with the welfare authorities as well as the recipient. Most jurisdictions provide an easy way for payors and recipients to find out which periods, if any, the support obligation was assigned to the government. It is very important to find this out before beginning your court case, so that if government rights are affected, you can involve them in the case. If you don't, and your support order is changed to the government's detriment, you may find yourself back in court facing a request by the government to overturn the part of the order affecting it.

Enforcement

People bound by court orders and agreements are expected to obey them. If they don't, the law provides enforcement mechanisms. For example, if one ex-partner is required to transfer a piece of property to the other and fails to do so, steps can be taken to make this happen. The same applies to lump sums that form part of a matrimonial property order or agreement. If you need advice about how to compel your ex-partner to comply with the property terms of your order or agreement, consult a lawyer.

Orders dealing with matrimonial property are usually one-time orders that involve a single transaction. Once the transaction is completed, there is no more need to enforce the order. In contrast, matters such as support, custody, and access can be more challenging to enforce because these orders last much longer and involve many transactions. For example, if support is to be paid monthly, there is a separate enforceable debt accruing each month. Similarly, if a parent is to have access visits with his/her children twice weekly, each scheduled visit is a separate occurrence that can require enforcement. Family law provides enforcement mechanisms to help parents get what their court orders and agreements entitle them to.

Support enforcement

Almost every jurisdiction in North America (and many other countries) has a government-operated support enforcement agency responsible for the collection and enforcement of support. All of these agencies will collect child support, and some will also collect spousal support. The agency usually receives the support payments by way of automatic wage deduction from the support payor's employment income. If the payor is self-employed, he/she is required to send the support payments to the enforcement agency. The agency then sends the money to the support recipient.

There are many advantages to having support enforced by a government agency. There is generally no fee payable by either party, although a delinquent payor may be required to pay enforcement fees or court costs to the agency. Secondly, the enforcement agency keeps accurate records of amounts owing and paid. Thirdly, and most importantly, the enforcement agency has a variety of enforcement tools and powers to locate delinquent payors and compel payment. Many agencies have the authority to garnishee bank accounts, pensions, employment insurance payments, and income tax refunds. They can seize and sell property owned by defaulting payors. In many places they have the authority to suspend driver's licences, hunting and fishing licences, and even passports. An enforcement agency can also ask the court to send a defaulting payor to jail if the payor is unable to prove a genuine inability to pay the support owed.

Not all parents use the services of a government support enforcement agency. If your support terms are in an agreement rather than a court order, and your support rights have not been assigned to the welfare authorities, there is no requirement that your support be collected by the enforcement agency. Many parents enter into private support agreements, and the payor makes support payments directly to the recipient. However, if you have an agreement and would like to have the enforcement agency handle the collection and enforcement of support, this may be possible. For example, some jurisdictions allow a support recipient or payor to file a support agreement with the court and then file it with the enforcement agency so it can be enforced as if it were a court order.

Conversely, some parents with court orders would prefer to deal with each other directly rather than have payments flow through a government enforcement agency. If you and your ex-partner have a court order that has been automatically filed with the enforcement agency, and the support rights have not been *assigned* to the welfare authorities, the law might permit you to withdraw from the agency. In some jurisdictions, the right to withdraw belongs only to the support recipient. In others, the order cannot be withdrawn unless both parties agree. If you have questions about this, contact your local support enforcement agency or consult a family law lawyer.

If your support order or agreement is registered with an enforcement agency, it is *very important* that all support payments be made through the agency. If you are a support payor, *do not* make support payments directly to the recipient, as the agency will not know about these payments and will not credit your account for them. Any payments made to the recipient directly might be considered gifts, or loans, or property settlements — but if you want them to count as support, you will have to prove they were intended to be support. If the support recipient denies receiving the funds, or claims they were paid for some other purpose, the court will have to decide whether to credit your support account based on the evidence presented by each party. Why take unnecessary risks and open the door to potential disagreements with your ex-partner and further court proceedings? If you and your ex-partner insist on giving and receiving support payments directly (but I am urging you *not* to), you should consider withdrawing your case from the enforcement agency. If you don't withdraw, be sure to keep written proof that you *both agreed* to the amount and purpose of each direct payment. Both parties should also notify the enforcement agency of these payments if you want them to count as support.

What if each parent lives in a different province, state, or country? In these circumstances, it is usually possible to enforce support obligations using inter-jurisdictional reciprocal enforcement laws. Canada, the United States, the United Kingdom, and a number of other countries have reciprocity agreements enabling the courts in one jurisdiction to enforce and vary support orders from another jurisdiction. If you have questions about how to obtain, vary, or enforce a support order when the other party resides in another province, state, or country, contact a family law lawyer for assistance.

Custody enforcement

Enforcement of custody orders often involves the police. If a parent has been granted custody of a child and the other parent is withholding the child, the police can be asked to assist the custodial parent in getting the child back. In some places, it will be necessary to obtain a court order directing the police to search for, locate, and return the child to the custodial parent. In addition, a parent who violates the other parent's custody rights can face the prospect of being criminally charged with child abduction.

If a child has been taken to another province, state, or country, the Convention on the Civil Aspects of International Child Abduction (called the Hague Convention) may be useful in securing the child's return. Every Canadian province and American state, and many other countries, are signatories to this convention. Each signatory state has a central authority responsible for bringing a court proceeding in the place where the child has been taken, so that an order for the return of the child can be made. If you need information or assistance regarding the Hague Convention, contact a family law lawyer. You may also find these Web sites helpful:

www.hcch.net/index_en.php?act=text.display&tid=21
In Canada:
www.justice.gc.ca/en/ps/pad/resources/fjis/report/appendix_b.asp
In the United States:
www.travel.state.gov/family/abduction/hague_issues/hague_issues_578.html

Access enforcement

It can be very frustrating and upsetting for a noncustodial parent whose access rights are being denied by the custodial parent. You already know from Chapter 9 that it is generally inappropriate to stop paying child support as a way of compelling the custodial parent to respect your access rights. Unless a court grants you permission to suspend support payments, do not do it.

What options are available to enforce access? The most common step taken is to call the police. Depending on the wording of your court order, the law where you live, the policies in effect at your local police department, and the particular circumstances in your case, this might be a helpful option. Some police departments require a court order directing their involvement before they will assist in the enforcement of an access order. Even if the court directs the police to enforce an access order, some police departments will not forcibly compel a child to go to the visit if the child is refusing to go.

The second most common step taken to enforce access is the bringing of a contempt motion. When a person violates a court order, that person is said to be in *contempt of court*. A contempt motion is an important court proceeding with serious consequences, and so the standard of proof used in criminal court is applied. If a court is satisfied beyond a reasonable doubt that a parent is deliberately refusing to comply with an access order, he/she can be found to be in contempt of court. The court can impose a variety of punishments on a parent who has been found to be in contempt of court. For example, the parent could be ordered to provide makeup compensating access visits. The parent might be ordered to pay a fine. In severe cases of repeated and blatant interference with access rights, a custodial parent could be sent to jail. It is important to note that if the parent goes to jail, the other parent may not automatically get custody of the child during the jail term; the child protection agency may be called in to assess the situation.

In most contempt motions I see, the parents do not disagree that the access is not occurring, but they disagree intensely on the *reasons* why access is not occurring. Parents in these cases typically accuse each other of a wide variety of inappropriate behaviour — everything from "brainwashing" the child to sexual assault to even bad cooking. Because contempt motions have a criminal law standard of proof and carry such serious consequences, it is highly recommended that you retain a lawyer before bringing a contempt motion. And if you are on the receiving end of a contempt motion, you also need a lawyer. Remember that in addition to whatever else happens at the motion, a court can order the unsuccessful party to pay the other party's costs.

There is one more step that I have seen noncustodial parents take in response to a denial of access: asking the court to give them custody. This is a most extreme route to take because the parent seeking custody will have to establish that it is in the child's best interests to switch homes and live with him/her. Although a denial of access is very serious, this is not the only factor that must be considered. The court must review *all* of the circumstances that go into a best interests analysis (see Chapter 6). Obviously, the fact that the child has not even had contact with the access parent for quite some time can make it difficult for that parent to prove that it would be best for the child to now live with him/her. Under no circumstances should a request to change custody be made without thorough legal advice from a family law lawyer.

Court orders are to be respected

There is no question that family courts everywhere are filled with angry and heartbroken parents whose custody, access, and support rights are being violated. Many parents spend years litigating in court to obtain orders resolving their disputes, only to find themselves back in court for many more years trying to enforce or vary those orders. Parents must understand that court orders are meant to be followed, and that serious consequences may result if they are not obeyed. If the principles of good conduct and maturity recommended in this book are followed, parents should be able to get on with the task of being parents rather than being litigants.

CHAPTER THIRTEEN

TEN TIPS FOR SUCCESS IN RESOLVING PARENTING DISPUTES

THE THEME OF THIS BOOK IS MATURITY. I believe the key to resolving parental disputes is for parents to behave in a civilized, reasonable, mature way with each other. Throughout the previous twelve chapters, I have attempted to show how mature behaviour can help you navigate your way through the family justice system. I have also pointed out some of the dire consequences that can result from immature behaviour.

If you are like many people who appear in my court, you will be thinking, "This is all well and good, but you don't know my ex-partner. I am doing all the right things. My ex-partner is the one creating all the problems." Believe me, I understand what you are thinking, but if you are truly trying to take a mature approach to your situation, you need to understand and accept the following important points:

1) There are two sides to every story. Each of you has a version of what happened in your relationship, and each of you firmly believes that your own versions are correct. No

amount of discussion or argument will change your opinion about the accuracy of your memories, and the same applies to your ex-partner. Ultimately, there is no way for anyone else to know for sure what actually happened and who did what to whom. More importantly, it isn't necessary to be right about what happened in the past in order to have a civilized co-parenting relationship with your ex-partner in the future. You can each agree to disagree about who was right and who was wrong and leave it at that.

2) Each of you probably identifies as the victim in the relationship. Whatever blame you want to cast at your ex-partner, he/she is very likely assigning at least as much blame to you. Instead of concentrating your energies on which ex-partner victimized the other most, you must focus on how to make sure your children are not victimized by your breakup. Their well-being matters more than yours. You and your ex-partner can go on to find new partners, but your children are not going to find new biological parents.

3) Finding a way to assign blame does nothing to solve your problems. Except in extreme cases, you are still going to have to deal with each other and the children for many years. You can each spend the rest of your lives trying to be vindicated for all that you have suffered, but in the meantime your children will be growing up in whatever atmosphere you and your ex-partner create for them. In the end, they will assess their childhoods not by deciding which parent was more blame-worthy in the family breakdown but rather by how well their parents protected them from their conflicts.

4) You cannot change your ex-partner, and he/she cannot change you. You are who you are — the same applies to your ex-partner. You chose to bring a new life into the world together — with all of your combined good qualities and faults. All the mudslinging, name-calling, and court proceedings in the world will not change that simple truth. However, you *can* change your own attitude, perspective, and behaviour. Only you can decide how you choose to react to your ex-partner's conduct. Even if in your opinion your ex-partner is behaving irresponsibly, you have an opportunity to

respond in a solution-oriented way rather than a vengeance-oriented way. You can deal with the issue at hand without necessarily escalating the conflict. This does *not* mean that you must accept abuse or put yourself or your children at risk of harm; it means that you can take the appropriate steps recommended by your lawyer, counsellor, and any other professionals you have turned to, without descending to your ex-partner's level. The expression "an eye for an eye, a tooth for a tooth" may have some relevance in a discussion of criminal justice, but it has absolutely no place in a discussion of co-parenting following separation. Good parenting is about raising healthy, happy children, *not* about getting even.

The above four points are, in my opinion, the fundamental cornerstones of mature parental behaviour following a separation. So here is my answer to the person who says, "I'm the good one. My ex-partner is the bad one": even if this is true, you still have an obligation, for your child's sake, to behave maturely and reasonably. This means at the very least getting legal advice from a family law lawyer before taking important steps affecting your ex-partner. It can also mean getting counselling to help you reinvent yourself from being a disappointed ex-partner to becoming a responsible co-parent. Counselling can also help you develop skills to respond appropriately to your ex-partner's conduct. If you respond the right way in each situation, you might be surprised at the effect this will have on your ex-partner. When you behave in a civilized and mature way with someone, you are, in a sense, role modeling for that person. I have seen many cases in which one parent's steadfast refusal to descend into the arena of retaliation and backstabbing literally shamed the other parent into improving his/her behaviour.

More importantly, when you show calmness, restraint, and fairness in your behaviour, you are also role modeling for your children, who see, hear, and remember much more than you probably realize. Children learn how to behave from their parents. If you truly believe that all of the problems are being caused by the other parent, it is even *more important than ever* that you behave with maturity. After all, it is better for a child to see one parent behaving properly than to see both parents behaving badly.

So, with that in mind, and once again reminding you to consult a lawyer for advice about your individual situation, here are my ten tips for success in dealing with your ex-partner.

1. Be child-focused.

Parents must learn to love their children more than they dislike each other. Children need peace more than their parents need to win. Make your child's well-being the focal point of every discussion you have with your ex-partner. Before taking a position on any issue, ask yourself, How will this affect my child? Ask your ex-partner to do the same. Never let a discussion with your ex-partner be about your needs or his/her needs; it should always be about your child's needs. If you cannot agree on which solution would best meet your child's needs, ask yourself how you and your ex-partner would have decided this issue had you remained together as a couple. In most cases, the answer would be to consult an expert. For example, if you and your ex-partner have a disagreement about your child's health, or educational needs, or extracurricular activities, you should both be meeting with your child's doctor, school, a family counsellor, or parenting coach. There are many professionals with special expertise to help parents resolve their disputes in a child-focused way. The first step to being a mature, responsible co-parent is to always put your children's needs ahead of your own.

2. Learn to distinguish between a bad partner and a bad parent.

The fact that your ex-partner was a bad partner does not necessarily mean that he/she is a bad parent. In my experience, most people who have been unfaithful to their spouses have actually treated their children very well. The way that a person treats his/her spouse in an unhappy relationship *when no children are present*[1] may not be a good indication of how that person treats his/her children. It can be extremely difficult for a parent who has been mistreated by the other parent to accept that the child might see that parent differently and have a good relationship with him/her. Your child is entitled to get to know the other parent in his/her own right and to have a relationship with the other parent that is independent from your own. Even if the other parent is flawed, and even if restrictions or limitations must be placed on his/her contact with the child, your child can still have a safe and beneficial relationship with that parent. If your feelings about the other parent are standing in the way of your child's relationship with him/her, you should seek help from a counsellor or therapist.

3. Never speak negatively to the child about the other parent.

Your child has a right to a loving relationship with each parent, free of any influence or brainwashing. Moreover, your child needs and deserves emotional permission from you to enjoy his/her relationship with the other parent. It is unfair and cruel to place your child in a conflict of loyalties and make him/her choose between you and your ex-partner, as this deprives the child of an important relationship. Keep your thoughts and opinions about the other parent to yourself; never share them with your child. Never draw your child into your disputes with the other parent. And while I'm at it, you should never criticize the other parent's family, new partner, or friends in front of your child. Nor should you tolerate your relatives, new partner, or friends denigrating or berating the other parent in front of your child. Make it clear to them that your child is to be shielded and protected from adult conflicts. Besides, it makes absolutely no sense to criticize people that your child is going to have a lot of contact with — what exactly do you want a child to do with this information? Most of the time a child will go right to the person who has been criticized and repeat everything you have said! Trust me, I've seen it happen thousands of times. One thing I have trouble understanding is why parents criticize each other's new partners. If you were attracted enough to your ex-partner to have a child with him/her, why does it surprise you that someone else finds him/her attractive? In most cases, a new partner had nothing to do with the breakup and is going to have considerable contact with your child. You gain nothing by making an enemy of that person.

4. Never argue or fight in front of your children.

No exceptions. If you and your ex-partner cannot behave civilly in front of your child, then don't be together in front of your child. It's that simple. I cannot understand why so many parents have trouble pretending to get along with each other for the few minutes it takes to pick up or return a child at access exchanges. It's called acting, and it's not that hard to do! Parents — even those who live together — pretend in front of their children all the time. It is even more important to do this after separation, because children need to be reassured that their lives will be happy and stable even though their parents live apart. Why are parents able to behave well in a courtroom in front of a judge (at least the vast majority do) but not in front of their own children? Don't they love their children enough to say "hello," "good-bye," and "have a nice day," and make small talk for the sake of keeping things peaceful and pleasant? Apparently not. This is shameful. There are lots of ways for parents to communicate with each other without the children being present: they can meet in person, or use telephones, faxes, letters, e-mails, and, of course, they can communicate through their lawyers. There is absolutely no good reason for parents to expose their children to their conflict. Parents who continually fail to heed this advice should be prepared to welcome the child protection authorities into their lives. (See Chapter 11.)

5. Listen to the other parent's point of view even if you don't agree with it.

If you are going to communicate directly with your ex-partner, remember that communicating with maturity starts with listening. You must learn to really hear what your ex-partner is saying, and understand his/her point of view. In any disagreement, try repeating back to your ex-partner what his/her position is, and the reasons why he/she is taking that position. I often do this in court and am frequently amazed by many people's inability to correctly repeat back to me what their ex-partners have just finished telling me only a few seconds before! For that matter, I am equally amazed at how often I am accused of saying things I did not say — thank heavens we have transcripts in court that record exactly what was said! The point I am making is that you cannot decide whether you agree with someone if you have not clearly understood what he/she is saying. You must put your emotions aside and listen with your brain. Even if you end up disagreeing with the other parent, you should at least be able to convey to him/her that you have understood his/her point of view. Many times I find that once two people have clearly understood the other's position, they are not as far apart as they first thought they were. Good listening skills are not acquired overnight, but post-separation counselling can be very helpful in speeding up the learning process.

6. Consider mediation before giving the decision-making power to a judge.

Too many parents react in a knee-jerk way to each other's conduct by running to family court without first getting legal advice or considering the impact of starting a court case. It is essential to consult a family law lawyer before taking any steps to resolve a conflict with an ex-partner. Your lawyer will explain your options and advise you on which one will best fit your situation. It may not be necessary to turn the decision-making power over to a judge. With the right help, you and your ex-partner may be able to arrive at compromises that will be better for your family than a court-imposed decision. Many thousands of parents have found mediation to be a beneficial problem-solving mechanism, so it is definitely worth exploring. For all the reasons given in Chapter 2, going to court should be a last resort, except for the special circumstances set out in Chapter 3.

7. Separate your financial issues from your parenting issues.

In any family breakdown, there are two types of issues to be resolved: financial issues and parenting issues. These are completely separate matters and should be dealt with that way. With the exception of the intersection that might occur between access and child support (see Chapter 9), you should not allow your discussions and disagreements over property and money to enter into your co-parenting relationship. Your relationship with your children should have nothing to do with financial transactions or property transfers. Even if your ex-partner's conduct regarding financial matters is making life difficult for you, this should not interfere with his/her role in your child's life. It can certainly be a challenge to behave civilly with someone whom you think is trying to cheat you financially, but the ability to keep parenting issues separate from financial matters is a hallmark of maturity.

8. Be flexible and reasonable in making access arrangements.

By far the greatest area of conflict between separated parents is that of organizing, carrying out, and enforcing access visits. Family courts everywhere are swamped with parents complaining of each other's frequent cancellations, lateness, and a myriad of other misbehaviours. In a great many of these cases, a little common sense and fairness from both parents would have gone a long way toward resolving the problem. Do your best to follow the four simple tips about access given in Chapter 12. Be flexible and reasonable in accommodating your ex-partner's work schedule and travel concerns, as well as changes in your child's routines. Be considerate when dealing with access on special occasions and during vacation periods. You never know when you might need your ex-partner to extend the same consideration to you. Remember that access schedules must be adjusted to accommodate changes in the parents' and children's lives. This is not only normal but is to be expected, so go with the flow, don't make a big deal out of every minor deviation from your access schedule, and be willing to make compromises for your child's sake.

9. Your children still see you as a family, so communicate!

As I have mentioned, you can be an ex-partner, but you are never going to be an ex-parent. If you truly accept that your children are innocent and bear no responsibility for your separation, then you know that they are entitled to be part of a family and to have their parents *behave* like family members, even though they live apart. Children who have contact with both parents need them to communicate with each other. I have had situations in which a child's health suffered because one parent didn't tell the other about the child's medical problem, so the child didn't get the proper medical attention in the other parent's care. This is unforgivable. When a child is going frequently from one parent's home to the other's, it is vital that each parent know about anything important that has happened to the child while in the other parent's care, especially an illness. It is also important for parents to have each other's addresses and telephone numbers, unless there is a very good reason to not disclose this information — and even in that case, there must be some way for parents to contact each other (for example, through a third party) in the event of an emergency. Parents should have equal rights to obtain information about their children from schools, doctors, and other service providers. Parents should have equal rights to attend important meetings such as parent-teacher interviews or key medical appointments. Both parents should be able to attend special events in the children's lives such as religious ceremonies, school events, sports tournaments, and music recitals. Even if there is a restraining order (or criminal court no-contact order) prohibiting contact, speak to your lawyer about the possibility of amending the order to permit at least some minimal form of communication regarding your child, even if it is in written form (for example, by using a communication book), or through a third-party intermediary.[2] Your children need you to know what's happening in their lives even when they're with the other parent. If possible, find a safe and legal way to make this happen.

10. Don't hesitate to get help.

Family breakdown is one of the most stressful and painful experiences anyone can go through. The challenge of overcoming a failed partnership while at the same time developing a good working relationship with an ex-partner can be overwhelming. You do not have to do this alone. There are specialized counsellors and therapists who can help you, your ex-partner, and your child. Many community organizations offer excellent programs to help separated parents and their children make the necessary transition from ex-partner to co-parent. There are social workers and parenting coaches with the expertise to help you and your ex-partner develop a workable parenting plan. There are many books that offer great ideas (see "Suggested Reading"). Speak to your family doctor about a referral to a counsellor or therapist. It's worth attending one meeting just to find out what services might be available to you and your family. Finally, remember that your family law lawyer is there to help you and can refer you to a number of community resources. Family law lawyers, like family court judges, know only too well that post-separation parental disputes are about much, much more than the law. Don't let the legal aspects of your dispute interfere with the critically important *human* aspects. If you do, you may be doing a disservice to your children.

Hope springs eternal in the judicial heart

Every day, my colleagues and I see the emotional carnage that results from high-conflict parental separations. We make the best decisions we can with the evidence we are given, which is often incomplete and almost always conflicting. We seldom find out the consequences of our decisions, and can only hope that the parents and children whose lives we touch have gone on to live happy and healthy lives. Although the work of a family court judge is sometimes discouraging, I am always heartened when I meet ex-partners who have learned to work together as a team for their children's benefit.

If you and your ex-partner have recently separated, please know that you are not alone. Millions have gone before you and have emerged from their pain as strong, emotionally healthy people. In the weeks and months following a separation, it is human nature to be confused and afraid. This does not always bring out the best in us. However, chances are that in time, your pain, anger, and fear will subside, and you will make great strides in your personal growth. I hope that the suggestions in this book will help speed up that process, so that you and your ex-partner can devote your energies to being the best parents — and co-parents — you can be. Remember, it's all about maturity!

---

1   It must be emphasized that parents who commit partner abuse in front of a child are also committing child abuse. It is extremely harmful to a child's emotional well-being to witness domestic violence. Therefore, in cases where domestic violence has occurred in the presence of a child, the perpetrator may well be considered to be lacking in good parenting skills. See Chapters 3 and 6 for more discussion regarding the impact of domestic violence in family law.

2   It is very important to respect the terms of a restraining order or other no-contact order imposed by a family court or criminal court. The circumstances of each case dictate the extent to which contact between the parents should be restricted. In some cases, a parent's right to be safe from abuse and harassment may necessitate a complete severance of communication. Orders that prohibit all forms of contact between ex-partners make it impossible for communication to occur, even if it pertains only to the child. If you are bound by a restraining order or no-contact order and wish to explore the possibility of establishing some means of communication with your ex-partner about your child, consult your lawyer.

SUGGESTED READING

Ackerman, Marc. *Does Wednesday Mean Mom's House or Dad's?: Parenting Together While Living Apart*. New York: John Wiley & Sons Inc., 1996.

Ahrons, Constance. *The Good Divorce: Keeping Your Family Together When Your Marriage Comes Apart*. New York: HarperCollins Publishers, 1995.

—. *We're Still Family: What Grown Children Have to Say About Their Parents' Divorce*. New York: HarperCollins Publishers, 2005.

Amato, Paul, and Alan Booth. *A Generation at Risk: Growing Up in an Era of Family Upheaval*. Cambridge: Harvard University Press, 2000.

—, David Johnson, Alan Booth, and Stacy J. Rogers. *Alone Together: How Marriage in America Is Changing*. Cambridge: Harvard University Press, 2007.

Antunes, Anne. *Divorce: A New Beginning: 10 Guidelines for a Good Ending*. Bloomington: Authorhouse, 2007.

Blackstone-Ford, Jann, and Sharyl Jupe. *Ex-Etiquette for Parents: Good Behaviour After a Divorce or Separation*. Chicago: Chicago Review Press, 2004.

Bonkowski, Sara. *Tots Are Non Divorceable: A Workbook for Divorced Parents and Their Children: Ages Birth to 5 Years*. Skokie: ACTA Publications, 1998.

Boyan, Susan Blyth, and Ann Marie Termini. *Cooperative Parenting and Divorce: Shielding Your Child From Conflict*. Kennesaw: Active Parenting Publishers, 1999.

Brown, Emily. *Affairs: A Guide to Working Through the Repercussions of Infidelity*. San Francisco: Jossey-Bass, 1999.

Coates, Christine, and Robert LaCrosse. *Learning From Divorce: How to Take Responsibility, Stop the Blame, and Move On*. San Francisco: Jossey-Bass, 2003.

Darnall, Douglas. *Divorce Casualties: Protecting Your Children From Parental Alienation.* Lanham: Taylor Trade Publishing, 1998.

Ellis, Carolyn. *The 7 Pitfalls of Single Parenting: What to Avoid to Help Your Children Thrive After Divorce.* Lincoln: IUniverse, 2007.

Emery, Robert. *The Truth About Children and Divorce: Dealing With the Emotions so You and Your Children Can Thrive.* New York: Plume, 2006.

Feuer, Jack. *Good Men: A Practical Handbook for Divorced Dads.* New York: Avon Books, 1997.

Garon, Risa. *Stop! In the Name of Love for Your Children: A Guide to Healthy Divorce.* Columbia: Children of Separation and Divorce Center, Inc., 2000.

Hannibal, Mary Ellen. *Good Parenting Through Your Divorce: The Essential Guidebook to Helping Your Children Adjust and Thrive.* New York: Marlowe & Company, 2007.

Hudgens, Marsha Lee. *Good People, Bad Marriages: Wisdom to Know, Freedom to Choose, Courage to Change.* Dickson: Estuary Publishing, 1996.

Johnston, Janet, and Vivienne Roseby. *In the Name of the Child.* New York: Free Press, 1997.

Mercer, Diana, and Marsha Kline Pruett. *Your Divorce Advisor: A Lawyer and Psychologist Guide You Through the Legal and Emotional Landscape of Divorce.* New York: Simon & Schuster, 2001.

Neumann, Diane. *Choosing a Divorce Mediator: A Guide to Helping Divorcing Couples Find a Competent Mediator.* New York: Owl Books, 1997.

Newman, George. *101 Ways to Be a Long-Distance Super-Dad . . . or Mom, Too!* Brandon: Robert D. Reed Publishers, 2006.

Ricci, Isolina. *Mom's House, Dad's House: A Complete Guide for Parents Who Are Separated, Divorced, or Remarried.* New York: Simon & Schuster, 1997.

Shields, Richard, Judith Ryan and Victoria Smith. *Collaborative Law: Another Way to Resolve Family Disputes*. Toronto: Carswell, 2003.

Stoner, Katherine. *Divorce Without Court: A Guide to Mediation and Collaborative Divorce*. Berkeley: NOLO, 2006.

Tesler, Pauline, and Peggy Thompson. *Collaborative Divorce: The Revolutionary New Way to Restructure Your Family, Resolve Legal Issues, and Move on With Your Life*. New York: ReganBooks, 2006.

Thayer, Elizabeth, and Jeffrey Zimmerman. *The Co-parenting Survival Guide: Letting Go of Conflict After a Difficult Divorce*. Oakland: New Harbinger Publications, 2001.

Thomas, Shirley. *Parents Are Forever: A Step-By-Step Guide to Becoming Successful Coparents After Divorce*. Longmont: Springboard Publications, 2004.

—. *Two Happy Homes: A Working Guide for Parents & Stepparents After Divorce and Remarriage*. Longmont: Springboard Publications, 2005.

—, and Dorothy Rankin. *Divorced But Still My Parents: A Helping Book About Divorce for Children and Parents*. Longmont: Springboard Publications, 1998.

Wallerstein, Judith, and Joan Kelly. *Surviving the Breakup: How Children and Parents Cope With Divorce*. New York: Basic Books, 1996.

Warshak, Richard. *Divorce Poison: Protecting the Parent-Child Bond From a Vindictive Ex*. New York: ReganBooks, 2001.

Webb, Stuart, and Ronald Ousky. *The Collaborative Way to Divorce: The Revolutionary Method That Results in Less Stress, Lower Costs, and Happier Kids — Without Going to Court*. New York: Hudson Street Press, 2006.

Williamson, Jack, and Mary Ann Salerno. *Divorce: 6 Ways to Get Through the Bad Times for Good*. Falls Church: Bridge Builder Media, 2001.

Wittmann, Jeffrey. *Custody Chaos, Personal Peace: Sharing Custody With an Ex Who Is Driving You Crazy*. New York: Perigee, 2001.

INDEX